PAUL HOLLYWOOD'S
—BRITISH BAKING—

For Alex

PAUL HOLLYWOOD'S
—BRITISH BAKING—

PHOTOGRAPHY BY PETER CASSIDY

BLOOMSBURY
LONDON · NEW DELHI · NEW YORK · SYDNEY

Recipes listed overleaf

NOTE

My baking times in the recipes are for conventional ovens. If you are using a fan-assisted oven, you will need to lower the oven setting by around 10–15°C. Ovens vary, so use an oven thermometer to verify the temperature and check your bakes towards the end of the suggested cooking time.

RECIPES

BREADS

SWEET YEASTED BREADS

CAKES & TEABREADS

BISCUITS & TRAYBAKES

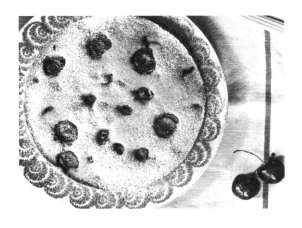

INTRODUCTION

I've been lucky enough to work all over the country as a baker, and everywhere I go, I see a passion for baking. I like to find out what people bake at home – and they love to tell me. Sometimes I learn about the cakes their grandmother made or they give me a family recipe. Each generation tweaks the recipe a bit to make it their own, but it retains the character of the original. You can almost trace a family's history through a recipe that's been handed down through the generations.

In the same way that families have their own baking tradition, so do the different parts of the British Isles – and to celebrate this diversity, the recipes in this book are divided up by area. I hope you'll turn to the chapter for the place where you live and think, 'Oh, I remember that,' or 'I never thought of cooking that, I'll give it a go.' But I also hope that you'll try the cakes, pies, puddings, breads and biscuits of other regions too, and find some new favourites. The first time you make a recipe, it's best to stick to it closely, but afterwards you might like to change it and make it your own, perhaps even creating a new tradition.

The charm and variety of baking in Scotland, England, Wales and Ireland is reflected in some of the old names. In this book you'll find huffkins, chudleighs and churdles; wiggs and fairings; plough pudding and fidget pie; bara brith and petticoat tails. Often the stories behind these names feature bakes that came about by accident – when a cook misinterpreted a recipe, perhaps, or when something was dropped – and miraculously tasted wonderful. Or they denote a moment in history, such as Henry VIII finding Anne Boleyn and her ladies-in-waiting tucking into little pastries and naming them 'Maids of Honour' on the spot. Whether the stories are true or not, they tell us something about our past and the significant role that baking has played in people's lives.

Although the baking of the British Isles is surprisingly diverse for a relatively small area, I have always been struck by the similarities from region to region too. Everywhere you go, you'll find common threads, such as griddle baking, steamed puddings, raised pies and enriched breads. Small adjustments give these things their regional character.

In the North of England, for example, they like their breads, pies and cakes to be baked darker than in the South, while in the Southwest, baking tends to be that little bit more refined than elsewhere.

I find it fascinating to look at the history of baking in this country and discover how these similarities and differences arose. Long ago, the local baker determined how things were done and people would come to think that was the way they should be done. Bakers liked to keep their recipes secret, as they weren't keen to encourage their customers to bake at home. Many of the variations you find in domestic cooking are interpretations of what was on sale at the local bakery.

Fundamentally, baking relies on a few simple ingredients: flour, fat, perhaps eggs, a raising agent such as yeast or baking powder and, for sweet bakes, sugar. In medieval times, wholemeal flour and flour made from other grains, such as rye, were standard for everyone except the wealthy. It was not until the Georgian era that refined white flour became relatively affordable. Flour grown in the British Isles is quite weak, which makes it ideal for cakes and biscuits, less so for bread.

In Scotland and the North, oats and barley were the dominant grains. Although barley is much less common now, oats still feature strongly — in Scottish oatcakes (page 290) and Yorkshire parkin (page 177), for example. Cakes were originally yeasted breads made of wheat, which is why there is still some confusion with names: saffron cake (page 41) and lardy cake are in fact what we think of as breads, because they are raised with yeast. In the North, round breads used to be known as cakes — so we still have stottie cakes (page 162), which would be considered rolls, baps or buns elsewhere in the country.

It is easy to see how the geography and farming of an area have shaped its baking traditions. Whether you used butter or lard in your cooking would have depended partly on income but also on the local farmland. In the Southwest, where there was good grazing for cows, butter and milk were plentiful, resulting in richer breads, cakes and biscuits. In regions such as East Anglia, where every smallholder kept a pig, lard was the fat of choice. Cheap and nutritious, it was also a means of using every last bit of the animal.

In the Southwest, cider, apples and clotted cream all find their way into baking, while in Kent, cherries are used in cakes and puddings to an extent that you simply don't find elsewhere. Scotland has virtually built its baking on oats, which grow so well in its cool, wet climate, and in Ireland the potato plays a unique role in breads and other baked goods. But some of the ingredients that play the biggest part in adding flavour and character to our baking are not indigenous at all.

Take sugar, for example. It's hard to imagine life without it but, until sugar cane was first imported from Barbados in the early 17th century, we had to rely on honey – a seasonal, costly ingredient – for sweetness. The availability of sugar changed everything, and Britain's dominance of the Caribbean gave us the monopoly on it for over a century. The dark side of sugar is that it was, of course, built on the slave trade.

Sugar remained expensive until the 19th century. Surprisingly, it is Napoleon we have to thank for the drop in price. When the British enforced a trade blockade during the Napoleonic Wars, he encouraged sugar beet production in France. Eventually this started to be cultivated in various parts of the British Isles too, though we still imported much of our sugar from the colonies. Suddenly everything was sweetened, from cups of tea to children's treats. Sugar was now a necessity rather than a luxury, becoming so cheap that it went from being the preserve of the rich to one of the mainstays of the working-class diet.

Yet, even before we had sugar to sweeten our bakes, we had dried fruit. It's impossible to imagine British baking without currants, raisins and sultanas. Eccles cakes, curd tarts, teabreads, mince pies, fruit cakes – these are uniquely British. Perhaps the key to why we've always used so much dried fruit is that it keeps for ages and is easy to transport. It was brought back to Britain by the Crusaders and became a flourishing trade in Tudor times – the classic English plum pudding was invented at the end of the 16th century. By the mid-19th century, dried fruit was cheap enough to be available to everyone. It was in the Victorian era that Christmas became widely celebrated in the way we know today, with all the festive baking and dried fruit consumption that entails.

Spices were another import that helped shape the character of our baking. Brought into ports such as Liverpool, Whitehaven, London and Bristol, they have had a tremendous impact on our cooking. One of the strengths of our cuisine is that we've never been afraid to borrow from other cultures, taking a little bit of this and a little bit of that to brighten things up. So it was with spices such as ginger, cinnamon, mace, nutmeg and caraway. Gradually, these imports bled into indigenous recipes and became part of the blueprint of British baking. In the past, spices like these not only added flavour but were also a useful way to disguise the strong taste of the yeast, or barm, which was taken from the top of beer.

In early days, our baking was dominated by the griddle, or bakestone. Every household would have had one, and they led to a rich seam of griddle cakes: crumpets, muffins, pikelets, Welsh cakes, oatcakes, boxty, to name just a few. This method of cooking was common throughout the country, but it is in Wales, Ireland, Scotland and the North that the tradition was strongest, and where many of our surviving griddle cakes hail from today. In these areas, wheat was less common, and grains such as barley and oats were not as easily made into breads, so the solution was to cook them on the griddle, often as pancakes. I love this kind of baking – it not only tastes good but it feels like a link with our past.

Other traditions have survived less well, and some of the recipes in this book represent a way of eating that has almost vanished – the Sussex churdles on page 71, for example, which are little hand-raised hot-water crust pies, filled with bacon, liver and apple; or the oatmeal drop scones (page 228), where oatmeal is soaked in buttermilk before being mixed with flour and egg and cooked on a griddle. Others rely on ingredients that we don't use much these days, notably lard and suet. Once staples, these ingredients fell out of favour during the second half of the 20th century because of health concerns, but now there's evidence that trans fats, found in margarines, are the real enemy.

We've held on to suet to some extent, adding it to steamed puddings and mince pies, but lard is much less common. It's making a sneaky comeback amongst chefs, however, who are rediscovering its great cooking qualities. If you bake from this book, I can promise you that you will learn to love lard. It makes wonderfully short, crisp pastry, though it's best with some butter added for flavour. It contains less saturated and more unsaturated fat than butter and has no trans fats. Suet, too, is not a fat we should be frightened of. In contrast to lard, it makes a soft pastry, which is why it is ideal for steamed puddings.

British baking suffered a few hard knocks in the 20th century: first during the Second World War, when rationing hit hard, persisting long after the war was over, and then with the rapid spread of convenience foods that followed. But look at us now – we're baking more than ever and, most importantly, the younger generation is happy to bake.

One reason why there's been a revival of interest in baking may be because it's more accessible than other types of cooking: what child hasn't started off learning to cook by making a few fairy cakes? Most of our baking recipes are based on ingredients that you probably already have in a kitchen cupboard. And, stemming more from a domestic tradition than a professional one, our bakes tend to be simple, quick and wholesome, with no difficult techniques to master.

We're pretty relaxed about recipes, and everyone is free to interpret them how they like, whether cooking professionally or at home. In other European countries it's quite different, with strict guidelines on how things should be done. In France, for example, the famous Opera cake has to have seven layers or it's simply not an Opera cake; in Germany the rules for making Black Forest gâteau are very strict, and professional bakers can lose their status as Konditormeister if they don't stick to them.

Of course, this doesn't mean we don't argue about how things should be done. There's plenty of debate about authenticity, provenance and the merits of different recipes. Very often there simply isn't a definitive answer and one interpretation is as valid as the next – we've never been good at defining and categorising our recipes, preferring a more casual approach. What really matters is that we are continuing a centuries-old tradition of adapting and developing recipes to suit what we have to hand. That's not to say we can stint on quality. Since the Second World War, we've got used to 'That'll do', instead of 'I'll buy the best'. As the recipes in this book demonstrate, British baking isn't lavish or expensive, but it does rely on an appreciation of decent ingredients.

I don't claim that this book is a comprehensive guide to the subject of British baking. I haven't included some staples such as mince pies and Victoria sponge, which don't belong to a specific area: the recipes are a combination of personal favourites, classics that simply couldn't be left out, bakes that have almost vanished but deserve to be better known, and new ones that I've developed using regional ingredients.

I hope that you'll enjoy discovering new bakes in British Baking, as much as I did when researching it. And even more than that, I hope that this book will help keep our regional baking traditions alive. If it starts a debate about exactly what those traditions are, then that means it has done its job.

EQUIPMENT

You won't need any fancy equipment for the recipes in this book. Many of them require little more than a mixing bowl, a wooden spoon and a baking tray. Even when something slightly more specialist is called for, such as a steamer or a griddle, it's easy to improvise if necessary.

One thing I find absolutely essential is a good set of digital scales. These are relatively inexpensive and, because you can put your mixing bowl on them and re-set them to zero, you can weigh everything directly into the bowl, which makes life easier.

I also recommend using an oven thermometer. Domestic ovens are notoriously inaccurate and, if an oven isn't cleaned often, accumulated grease and dirt can affect the heat level and ventilation, creating hot spots. Set the oven to 200°C/Gas 6, then check the temperature with your thermometer after 10 minutes. Remember, too, that ovens need to be cleaned and serviced regularly. Your bakes will be all the better for it.

Rolling out pastry is much easier if you have a decent rolling pin. I suggest you go for a traditional, long wooden one. A heavy rolling pin also means that you don't have to put too much weight on it. I have a sieve, of course, but I rarely sift flour. It's only necessary when you are folding flour into a mixture and need to add as much air as possible.

You will need two baking trays for many of the rolls and biscuits in this book. It's worth spending a bit extra to get robust, heavy-duty ones that don't buckle in the heat of the oven. They'll last for ages. Similarly, buy good-quality tart tins, cake tins, loaf tins and bun and muffin trays.

A sharp serrated knife is always handy, particularly when it comes to slicing breads, cakes and pies. And you will need a set of pastry cutters for cutting out pastry rounds, scones and biscuits, a pastry brush for glazing, and one or two wire cooling racks.

All the griddle baking in this book can be done in a large, heavy-based frying pan, but if you enjoy this type of baking, consider treating yourself to a proper cast-iron griddle, known as a girdle in Scotland and a bakestone in Wales. A good one will probably last several lifetimes, so you can even leave it to your grandchildren.

THE — SOUTHWEST

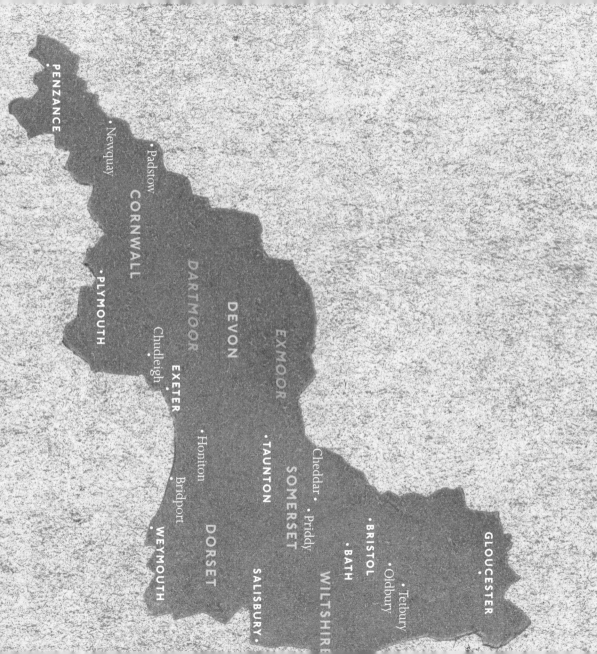

Clotted cream, Cheddar cheese, strawberries, saffron cake, pasties, cider – the West Country is home to some of our greatest culinary treasures. Spring arrives that little bit earlier here than anywhere else in the British Isles, meaning that fruit and vegetables are ready for market sooner.

Dairy cattle produce milk with a particularly high butterfat content, thanks to the area's lush pastures. The resulting butter and cream are second to none, while cheeses include not just Cheddar but also Dorset Blue Vinny, Double Gloucester, Cornish Yarg and various new cheeses created by enterprising small producers.

Old breeds of pigs, such as the Gloucester Old Spot, the Large Black and the rare British Lop might, if they are lucky, still root around in the apple orchards that produce the region's cider. And, of course, fishing boats set out daily from Cornwall, Devon and Dorset to bring us the fish and shellfish for which the coastline is justly famous.

For bakers, the West Country is a happy place to be. For starters, it's the home of the cream tea – that perfect mid-point to a summer afternoon, preferably eaten in a country garden under the shade of a large tree. Strawberry jam and thick clotted cream are the vital components, to be spread on freshly baked scones or used to fill a Devonshire split. Cream or jam first on your scone? It's your call, though in Devon they tend to go for cream first, in Cornwall jam.

Although much of the baking of the Southwest is simple and rustic in character, the elegant city of Bath has created some more refined products, thanks to its role as a social hub of Georgian society. Bath Olivers, Bath buns, Sally Lunns and seed cake all come from the city. Bath Olivers are very hard to reproduce at home, so you won't find them in this chapter, but I have included the Sally Lunn (page 38), as well as the wonderfully named Dorset wiggs (page 47) and Bristol Mothering buns (page 48).

Arguably the region's most famous baked product is the Cornish pasty, which was recently awarded protected origin status by the EU. You simply can't beat a good pasty and in this chapter you'll find two: the classic Cornish pasty on page 22 and the lesser-known but equally fine Somerset Priddy oggie on page 26.

This is the original portable meal, eaten by Cornish tin miners and farm labourers. The pastry had to be robust to make it portable, and it was quite common to have a savoury filling at one end, sweet at the other. It now has protected status and must be made in Cornwall. The vegetables need to be cut thinly so they almost melt into the meat on cooking, and the crimping is all-important. I was told that you need 21 crimps to make a proper pasty.

PASTRY

450g plain flour

½ tsp salt

115g cold lard, diced

75g cold unsalted butter, diced

About 90ml ice-cold water

1 egg, lightly beaten, to glaze

FILLING

1 large onion

120g swede

1 large floury potato, such as King Edward or Maris Piper

400g beef skirt

50g butter

Salt and pepper

EQUIPMENT

A 24cm plate (to use as a guide)

STEP PHOTOGRAPHS OVERLEAF

1. To make the pastry, mix the flour and salt in a large bowl, add the lard and butter and rub in with your fingertips until the mixture resembles breadcrumbs. Stir in enough water to make a fairly firm dough, then knead briefly until smooth. Shape into a ball, wrap in cling film and chill for at least 30 minutes.

2. For the filling, slice the onion finely; cut the swede and potato into small, thin strips; keep each separate. Cut the beef into small, thin pieces and divide into 5 portions.

3. Heat the oven to 200°C/Gas 6. Divide the pastry into 5 equal pieces. Roll each out on a lightly floured surface to a 3mm thickness and cut out a 24cm circle, using a plate as a guide.

4. Scatter a scant layer of swede on the pastry semi-circle, leaving a 1cm border. Add a similar layer of potato, season lightly and top with some onion. Repeat the swede and potato layers, seasoning as you go. Check the pasty will close, then add the beef. Add a final layer of onion, season and dot with butter.

5. Brush the pastry border with a little beaten egg, then close the lid of the pasty, making sure that the edges meet. Press together firmly and then crimp the edges together by pinching all the way round between your thumb and forefinger.

6. Fill and seal the remaining circles of pastry in the same way. Place the pasties on 2 baking trays and cut 2 small slits in the middle of each one. Brush the pastry with beaten egg. Bake for 20 minutes, then lower the oven setting to 160°C/Gas 3 and bake for 30 minutes longer. Best eaten hot from the oven.

Gently kneading the pastry into a ball, ready to wrap and chill before rolling out.

Rolling out a portion (one-fifth) of the rested pastry on a lightly floured surface to a round, 3mm thick.

Cutting out a neat circle from the pastry round, using an upturned 24cm plate as a guide.

Laying one half of the pastry circle over the rolling pin (this will make it easier to fill and close the pastry).

Layering the finely cut vegetables on the pastry, leaving a 1 cm border free around the edge.

Scattering the final layer of sliced onion on top of the beef.

Folding the uncovered semi-circle of pastry over the filling, bringing the edges together neatly, to close the pasty.

Pinching the edges of the pastry together between your thumb and forefinger to crimp and seal.

Don't be fooled by the name, this isn't an ancient recipe but was invented in 1968 by a pub landlord in the village of Priddy, in Somerset. It makes use of local ingredients – pork, cheese, apple and bacon – and deserves its status as an instant classic. Oggy is a West Country word for pasty.

PASTRY

450g plain flour

½ tsp salt

115g cold lard, diced

75g cold butter, diced

25g Parmesan cheese, finely grated

70–80ml ice-cold water

1 egg, lightly beaten, to glaze

FILLING

300g pork tenderloin

150g smoked streaky bacon

1 medium cooking apple

1 large onion, coarsely grated

75g mature Cheddar cheese, grated

2 tbsp chopped parsley

Salt and pepper

EQUIPMENT

A 24cm plate (to use as a guide)

1. To make the pastry, mix the flour and salt in a large bowl, add the lard and butter and rub them in with your fingertips until the mixture resembles breadcrumbs. Stir in the Parmesan, then add enough water to make a fairly firm dough. Knead briefly until smooth, then shape into a ball, wrap in cling film and chill for at least 30 minutes.

2. For the filling, cut the pork and smoked bacon into roughly 5mm pieces. Peel, core and quarter the apple. Slice it thinly, then cut the slices in half. Combine the pork, bacon, apple and onion in a bowl. Add the cheese and parsley and mix well, seasoning with a little salt and some pepper.

3. Heat the oven to 200°C/Gas 6. Divide the pastry into 5 equal pieces. Roll each out on a lightly floured surface to a 3mm thickness and cut out a 24cm circle, using a plate as a guide.

4. Divide the filling between the pastry circles, placing it in the centre of each one. Brush the border of the pastry with beaten egg, then bring both sides of the pastry up so they meet at the top and press together to seal. Crimp the join by pinching it all the way along between your thumb and forefinger.

5. Place the pies on 2 baking trays, brush with beaten egg and bake for 20 minutes. Lower the oven setting to 160°C/Gas 3 and bake for 30 minutes longer. Leave to cool for a few minutes before eating.

BAKED SOMERSET BRIE

SERVES 4–6

This is a great way to enjoy one of the excellent Bries produced in Somerset and Cornwall. A medium (13–15cm diameter) cheese is wrapped in Parma ham, then in an enriched bread dough, and baked. Choose a slightly firm Brie for this recipe. Don't be tempted to cut it as soon as it comes out of the oven, or the molten Brie will flood out, leaving you with an empty shell. If you serve it just very slightly warm, though, you will have a deliciously oozy cheese.

ENRICHED BREAD DOUGH

250g strong white bread flour
1 tsp salt
7g sachet instant yeast
50g unsalted butter, softened
1 medium egg, lightly beaten, plus an extra beaten egg to glaze
135ml warm full-fat milk

FILLING

180g Parma ham (or British air-dried ham)
3 tbsp cranberry sauce
1 whole Somerset or Cornish Brie (about 500g)

1. Put the flour into a large bowl and add the salt on one side, the yeast on the other. Add the butter, egg and two-thirds of the milk, then turn the mixture round with the fingers of one hand. Add the remaining milk a little at a time, continuing to mix until you have taken in all the flour from the side of the bowl and the dough is soft and slightly sticky; you might not need all the milk.

2. Transfer the dough to a lightly floured surface and knead for 5–10 minutes. Initially it will be sticky but it will become easier to work as you knead. When it feels smooth and silky, put it into a lightly oiled bowl, cover and leave to rise for about an hour, until doubled in size.

3. Heat the oven to 200°C/Gas 6. Turn the dough onto a lightly floured surface and fold it in on itself a few times to knock out the air. Now roll out to a large circle, about 5mm thick.

4. Lay half the Parma ham on the centre of the dough circle, then spread the cranberry sauce over the ham. Place the Brie on top and use the remaining ham to cover the cheese. Lift the edges of the dough over the filling and stretch to encase the cheese. Press the edges together to seal, trimming off any excess.

5. Turn the Brie parcel over, so the join is underneath, and place it on a baking tray. Brush with the beaten egg. Using the back of a sharp knife, score a criss-cross pattern over the top of the Brie parcel. Bake for 20–25 minutes, until golden brown. Allow to cool until just warm before serving.

OLDBURY GOOSEBERRY PIES

MAKES 6

Gooseberries make one of the best summer pies, with plenty of sharp-sweet juices to soften and enrich the crust. These little pies from Oldbury in Gloucestershire are made with hot-water pastry. It's a sturdy pastry and the lard content helps create a barrier that seals the juices in. Be sure to use the pastry straight away; if you leave it to cool completely, it will start to set and become crumbly.

HOT-WATER PASTRY

360g plain flour
80g strong white bread flour
½ tsp icing sugar
50g unsalted butter, diced
160ml water
80g lard, diced
1 egg, lightly beaten, to glaze

FILLING

6 tsp semolina
450g gooseberries, topped and tailed
85g caster sugar
85g light soft brown sugar

EQUIPMENT

An 18cm plate (to use as a guide)

STEP PHOTOGRAPHS OVERLEAF

1. To make the pastry, mix the flours and icing sugar in a large bowl, add the butter and rub it in lightly with your fingertips. Heat the water and lard in a small pan until the lard has melted and the water has just come to the boil. Pour the mixture onto the flour and stir with a wooden spoon until combined. Turn out onto a floured surface and knead briefly until smooth.

2. Set aside a quarter of the pastry, wrapped in cling film. Divide the rest into 6 balls. Roll out each one quite thinly on a lightly floured surface, then cut into an 18cm circle, using a plate as a guide. Keep the other balls covered with cling film as you work.

3. Once you have six 18cm circles, gather up the edges of each one to create the walls of the pie, pinching little pleats around the edge; they should be about 2–3cm high.

4. Sprinkle 1 tsp semolina over the base of each pastry case, then add the gooseberries. Mix the caster and brown sugars together and scatter over the fruit.

5. Divide the reserved pastry into 6 pieces and roll out each one to make a lid. Trim to fit the pies, then position over the filling and inside the pastry walls. Pinch the edges together to seal. Make a slit in the top of each pie to let the steam out.

6. Put the pies on a baking tray and refrigerate for a few hours or overnight to firm up, so they hold will their shape on baking.

7. Heat the oven to 200°C/Gas 6. Brush the pies with the beaten egg and bake for 20–30 minutes until the pastry is crisp and golden brown. Serve hot or cold, with lashings of thick cream.

Positioning the pastry lid over the gooseberry filling and inside the pastry walls.

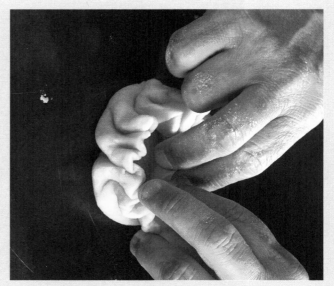

Gathering up the edges of the pastry circle and pinching them together in little pleats to form the walls of the pie.

Pinching the edges of the pastry lid and walls together to seal.

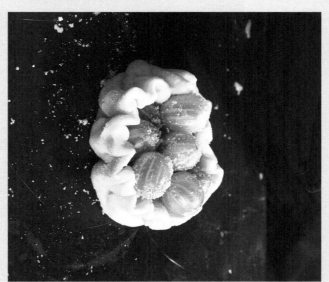

Sprinkling the mixed caster and brown sugar over the gooseberries in the pie cases.

PAUL HOLLYWOOD'S
— BRITISH BAKING LIVE TOUR —
Favourite recipes, from Cornish pasties to Bakewell tarts

NOVEMBER

THU	06	POOLE LIGHTHOUSE
FRI	07	READING HEXAGON
SAT	08	CARDIFF ST DAVIDS HALL
SUN	09	AYLESBURY THEATRE
MON	10	EASTBOURNE CONGRESS HALL
WED	12	TORQUAY PRINCESS THEATRE
THU	13	BATH FORUM
SUN	16	LIVERPOOL AUDITORIUM ECHO ARENA
MON	17	DUBLIN OLYMPIA
TUE	18	DUBLIN OLYMPIA
WED	19	BELFAST WATERFRONT
THU	20	GRIMSBY AUDITORIUM
FRI	21	BLACKBURN KING GEORGES HALL
SAT	22	CARLISLE SANDS
MON	24	DUNDEE CAIRD HALL
TUE	25	ABERDEEN MUSIC HALL
WED	26	SOUTHPORT THEATRE
THU	27	PRESTON GUILDHALL
SUN	30	BASINGSTOKE ANVIL

DECEMBER

TUE	02	HALIFAX VICTORIA
WED	03	BRADFORD ST GEORGES HALL
THU	04	LLANDUDNO VENUE CYMRU
FRI	05	BRIDLINGTON ROYAL HALL
SAT	06	WARWICK BUTTERWORTH HALL
SUN	07	STEVENAGE CONCERT HALL
MON	08	NORWICH THEATRE ROYAL

TICKETS & VIP MEET AND GREET PACKAGES AVAILABLE FROM:
PAULHOLLYWOOD.COM
TICKETMASTER.CO.UK / THETICKETFACTORY.COM / 0844 871 8803

PAUL HOLLYWOOD'S
— BRITISH BAKING LIVE TOUR —

Favourite recipes, from Cornish pasties to Bakewell tarts

NOVEMBER

THU	06	POOLE LIGHTHOUSE
FRI	07	READING HEXAGON
SAT	08	CARDIFF ST DAVIDS HALL
SUN	09	AYLESBURY THEATRE
MON	10	EASTBOURNE CONGRESS HALL
WED	12	TORQUAY PRINCESS THEATRE
THU	13	BATH FORUM
SUN	16	LIVERPOOL AUDITORIUM ECHO ARENA
MON	17	DUBLIN OLYMPIA
TUE	18	DUBLIN OLYMPIA
WED	19	BELFAST WATERFRONT
THU	20	GRIMSBY AUDITORIUM
FRI	21	BLACKBURN KING GEORGES HALL

SAT	22	CARLISLE SANDS
MON	24	DUNDEE CAIRD HALL
TUE	25	ABERDEEN MUSIC HALL
WED	26	SOUTHPORT THEATRE
THU	27	PRESTON GUILDHALL
SUN	30	BASINGSTOKE ANVIL

DECEMBER

TUE	02	HALIFAX VICTORIA
WED	03	BRADFORD ST GEORGES HALL
THU	04	LLANDUDNO VENUE CYMRU
FRI	05	BRIDLINGTON ROYAL HALL
SAT	06	WARWICK BUTTERWORTH HALL
SUN	07	STEVENAGE CONCERT HALL
MON	08	NORWICH THEATRE ROYAL

Brushing the pastry with beaten egg to glaze.

WHOLEMEAL SEEDED LOAF

MAKES 1 LARGE LOAF

One of my favourite flours is produced at Shipton Mill near Tetbury in the heart of the Cotswolds. The flour is still stoneground from local organic grain in the traditional way. It makes an unbeatable nutritious loaf that deserves to take pride of place on the table. Shipton Mill flour, and other organic stoneground flours, can be sourced online, or try your local deli or healthfood store.

500g stoneground strong
    wholemeal flour
7g salt
2 x 7g sachets instant yeast
3 tbsp olive oil
350ml water
50g sesame seeds
50g pumpkin seeds
50g sunflower seeds

STEP PHOTOGRAPHS OVERLEAF

1. Put the flour into a large bowl and add the salt on one side, the yeast on the other. Add the oil and three-quarters of the water, then turn with the fingers of one hand. Add the remaining water a little at a time, mixing until all the flour is taken in and you have a soft dough; you might not need all the water.

2. Oil the work surface to prevent sticking. Turn out the dough and knead for about 10 minutes, until smooth and silky. Lightly oil the bowl, return the dough to it and cover with cling film. Leave to rise for 1–2 hours, until at least doubled in size.

3. Line a baking tray with baking parchment. Combine the seeds and add half of them to the dough. Knead to knock out the air and incorporate the seeds. Transfer to a lightly floured surface and fold the dough inwards repeatedly until it is smooth.

4. To shape, flatten into a rectangle with a long side facing you. Fold each end into the middle, roll the dough up and turn it over so the seam is underneath. Roll it lightly, applying more pressure at the ends to create a long oval shape.

5. Spray the loaf all over with water. Scatter the remaining seeds over the surface and roll the loaf in the seeds so they cover it completely. Transfer to the lined baking tray, place in a clean plastic bag and leave to prove for about 45 minutes, until doubled in size. Heat the oven to 190°C/Gas 5.

6. Just before baking, snip deeply along the top of the loaf with scissors. Bake for 40 minutes or until the bread sounds hollow when tapped on the base. Transfer to a wire rack to cool.

Adding half of the mixed sesame, pumpkin and sunflower seeds to the risen dough.

Transferring the kneaded seeded dough to a lightly floured surface, ready for shaping.

Snipping deeply into the top of the dough along its length to create an attractive finish.

Punching down the dough with the knuckles to knock out the air.

Gently rolling the loaf back and forth, applying a little more pressure on the ends to create a long oval shape.

SALLY LUNN

MAKES 1 SMALL LOAF

This is basically a light brioche. The origin of the name is unclear, but one story suggests that it was brought to Bath in 1680 by a French Huguenot refugee, Solange Luyon, and the buns she subsequently sold in the streets around Bath Abbey became known by an anglicised version of her name, Sally Lunn. I remember as a child eating a version of this in Liverpool that included dried fruit and glacé icing, also known as a Sally Lunn.

275g strong white bread flour
1 tsp salt
2 tsp caster sugar
7g sachet instant yeast
30g unsalted butter, softened
1 large egg, beaten
120ml milk
2 tsp caster sugar, mixed with
  2 tsp milk, for brushing

EQUIPMENT
A deep 15cm round cake tin

1. Put the flour into a large bowl and add the salt and sugar on one side, the yeast on the other. Add the butter, egg and two-thirds of the milk, then turn the mixture round with the fingers of one hand. Add the remaining milk a little at a time, continuing to mix until you have taken in all the flour from the side of the bowl and the dough is soft and quite sticky; you might not need all the milk.

2. Transfer the dough to a lightly floured surface and knead for 5–10 minutes. Initially it will be sticky but it will become easier to work as you continue to knead. When the dough feels smooth and silky, put it into a lightly oiled bowl, cover and leave to rise for about 2–3 hours, until doubled in size.

3. Butter a deep 15cm cake tin. Tip the risen dough onto a lightly floured surface and fold it in on itself a few times to knock out the air, then shape it into a round.

4. Put the dough into the prepared cake tin, pressing it out gently so it reaches the side of the tin. Cover loosely with cling film and leave until doubled in size. Heat the oven to 200°C/Gas 6.

5. Remove the cling film and bake the loaf for 20 minutes, until it is well risen and golden brown on top. As soon as it is done, brush the top with the sugar and milk mixture to lend a very shiny glaze. Transfer to a wire rack and leave to cool. Serve sliced and buttered.

SAFFRON CAKE

MAKES 1 LARGE LOAF

Speckled with currants and candied peel, this is an enriched bread rather than a cake. Saffron was grown in Cornwall until the end of the 19th century. It gives the loaf not just its glorious golden colour but also a subtle, honeyed flavour. Spread with butter or clotted cream, saffron cake is a real treat; it also makes great toast.

½ tsp saffron strands
125ml milk
450g strong white bread flour
¼ tsp ground mixed spice
½ tsp salt
100g light soft brown sugar
7g sachet instant yeast
85g unsalted butter, diced
    and softened
150ml water
175g currants
1 tbsp finely chopped mixed
    candied peel

EQUIPMENT
A 1kg loaf tin

1. Place the saffron and milk in a pan and heat gently until just hot. Turn off the heat and leave to infuse for at least 2 hours.

2. Put the flour and spice in a bowl. Add the salt and sugar on one side, the yeast on the other. Add the butter and saffron milk and turn the mix with the fingers of one hand. Add the water a little at a time, mixing until all the flour is taken in and the dough is soft and slightly sticky; you might not need all the water.

3. Oil the work surface to prevent sticking. Turn out the dough and knead for at least 5 minutes, until smooth and no longer sticky. Lightly oil the bowl, return the dough to it and cover with cling film. Leave to rise until doubled in size – this will take anything from 1–3 hours. Butter a 1kg loaf tin.

4. Scrape the dough out onto a lightly floured surface and fold it inwards repeatedly until the air is knocked out and the dough is smooth. Knead in the currants and peel a handful at a time.

5. Form the dough into an oblong by flattening it out slightly and folding the sides into the middle. Roll the whole lot up: the top should be smooth with the seam running along the length of the base. Put the dough into the prepared tin.

6. Put the tin in a plastic bag. Leave to prove for about 2 hours, until the dough has doubled in size and springs back if gently prodded with your finger. Heat the oven to 200°C/Gas 6.

7. Bake the loaf for 20 minutes, then lower the setting to 180°C/Gas 4 and bake for another 20 minutes, until it is golden brown and sounds hollow when tapped underneath. Remove from the tin and cool on a wire rack.

One of the first things I remember eating was a Devonshire split. In Liverpool we used to take them one step further and use an iced finger bun. The alternative name for a Devonshire split is Chudleigh, presumably after the village of that name in Devon.

500g strong white bread flour
2 tsp salt
40g caster sugar
2 x 7g sachets instant yeast
40g unsalted butter, diced
  and softened
150ml milk
150ml water

FILLING
200ml double cream
100g strawberry jam
Icing sugar, for dusting

EQUIPMENT
Piping bag and large star nozzle

STEP PHOTOGRAPHS OVERLEAF

1. Put the flour in a large bowl. Add the salt and sugar on one side, the yeast on the other. Add the butter, milk and three-quarters of the water, then turn the mixture round with the fingers of one hand. Add the remaining water a little at a time, mixing until you have taken in all the flour and the dough is soft and slightly sticky; you might not need all the water.

2. Oil the work surface to prevent sticking. Knead the dough on it for at least 5 minutes, until smooth and no longer sticky. Lightly oil the bowl, return the dough to it and cover with cling film. Leave to rise for at least an hour, until doubled in size.

3. Line 2 baking trays with baking parchment. Scrape the dough out of the bowl onto a lightly floured surface and then fold it inwards repeatedly until all the air has been knocked out and the dough is smooth. Divide into 12 pieces.

4. Roll each piece into a ball by placing it into a cage formed by your hand on the work surface and moving your hand in a circular motion, rotating the ball rapidly.

5. Put the balls of dough on the prepared baking trays, spacing them slightly apart. Place each tray in a clean plastic bag and leave to prove for about 40 minutes, until the rolls have doubled in size. Heat the oven to 220°C/Gas 7.

6. Bake for 10–12 minutes, until the rolls are golden and sound hollow when tapped underneath. Place on a wire rack to cool.

7. Whip the cream until fairly stiff and put into a piping bag fitted with a large star nozzle. Score each cooled bun deeply through the middle, open it up and pipe in a line of cream. Spoon or pipe a thin line of jam alongside. Dust the buns with icing sugar.

Incorporating the remaining water into the dough until it is evenly combined, soft and slightly sticky.

Dividing the knocked-back dough into 12 equal pieces, ready for shaping.

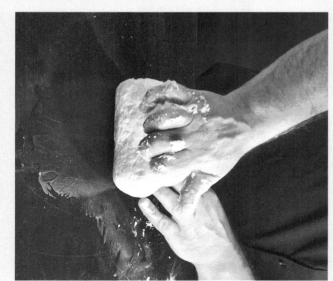

Kneading the dough by stretching the top away from you, then folding it back in repeatedly, turning it 45° after each 'stretch and tuck'.

Rolling each piece into a ball by placing it in a cage formed by your hand and moving the hand in a circular motion, rotating the ball rapidly.

Carefully scoring a deep cut into the bun with a sharp knife, to make room for the cream and jam filling.

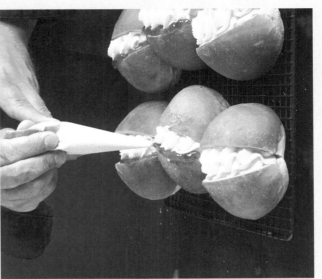

Piping a thin line of jam to one side of the cream, using a greaseproof paper piping bag with the tip snipped off.

The fully proved buns, expanded to twice their original size, ready for baking.

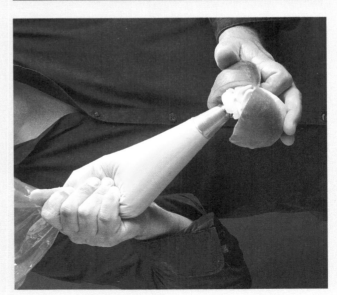

Piping a fluted line of cream into the bun, using a piping bag fitted with a large star nozzle.

DORSET WIGGS

MAKES 12

Wiggs, or whiggs, are light, plain teacakes, subject to regional variation. The Dorset wigg is a soft, sweet roll, subtly flavoured with nutmeg, mace and a touch of caraway. Originally they would have been made close to a brewery, using barm scraped off the top of the beer for the yeast. Sometimes this lent a strong flavour, so spices were added to the bread to mask it. These wiggs are lovely eaten still warm from the oven, or toasted, with butter and jam.

500g strong white bread flour
1 tsp salt
75g caster sugar
2 x 7g sachets instant yeast
¼ tsp ground cloves
¼ tsp ground mace
¼ tsp ground nutmeg
1 tsp caraway seeds
75g unsalted butter, diced
　and softened
150ml milk
150ml water

1. Put the flour in a large bowl and add the salt and sugar on one side, the yeast on the other. Add the spices, butter, milk and three-quarters of the water, then turn the mixture round with the fingers of one hand. Add the remaining water a little at a time, continuing to mix until you have taken in all the flour from the side of the bowl and the dough is soft and slightly sticky; you might not need all the water.

2. Coat the work surface with a little oil to prevent the dough sticking. Turn out the dough and knead for at least 5 minutes, until it is smooth and no longer sticky. Lightly oil the bowl, return the dough to it and cover with cling film. Leave to rise for at least an hour, until doubled in size.

3. Line 2 baking trays with baking parchment. Scrape the dough out of the bowl onto a lightly floured surface and fold it inwards repeatedly until all the air has been knocked out and the dough is smooth. Divide into 12 pieces.

4. Roll each piece into a ball by placing it in a cage formed by your hand on the work surface and moving your hand in a circular motion, rotating the ball rapidly.

5. Put the balls of dough on the prepared baking trays, spacing them slightly apart. Place each tray in a clean plastic bag and leave to prove for about 40 minutes, until the rolls have doubled in size. Heat the oven to 220°C/Gas 7.

6. Bake for 10–12 minutes, until the rolls are golden and sound hollow when tapped underneath. Cool slightly on a wire rack.

MOTHERING BUNS

A speciality of Bristol, these are still made by local bakers on the day before Mothering Sunday. Traditionally on this day, the Lent fast was relaxed. The buns used to be decorated with caraway or aniseed; today hundreds and thousands are used.

500g strong white bread flour
1 tsp salt
50g caster sugar
7g sachet instant yeast
50g unsalted butter, diced
　and softened
300ml water

ICING

200g icing sugar
2–3 tbsp water
6 tbsp hundreds and thousands

1.　Put the flour in a large bowl. Add the salt and sugar on one side, the yeast on the other. Add the butter and three-quarters of the water, then turn the mixture round with the fingers of one hand. Add the remaining water a little at a time, mixing until you have taken in all the flour and the dough is soft and slightly sticky; you might not need all the water.

2.　Oil the work surface to stop the dough sticking. Turn out the dough and knead for 5 minutes, or until smooth and no longer sticky. Lightly oil the bowl, return the dough to it and cover with cling film. Leave to rise for at least an hour, until doubled in size. Line 2 baking trays with baking parchment.

3.　Scrape the dough out of the bowl onto a lightly floured surface and fold it inwards repeatedly until all the air has been knocked out and the dough is smooth. Divide into 12 pieces.

4.　Roll each piece into a ball by placing it into a cage formed by your hand on the work surface and moving your hand in a circular motion, rotating the ball rapidly.

5.　Put the balls of dough on the prepared baking trays, spacing them slightly apart. (They should just touch each other when they have risen.) Place each tray in a clean plastic bag and leave to prove for about 40 minutes, until the rolls have doubled in size. Heat the oven to 220°C/Gas 7.

6.　Bake for 10–12 minutes, until the rolls are golden and sound hollow when tapped underneath. Transfer to a wire rack to cool.

7.　For the icing, mix the icing sugar with enough water to give a fairly thick but still pourable consistency. Dip the top of each roll into the icing and then into the hundreds and thousands.

STRAWBERRY AND PISTACHIO SHORTCAKES

MAKES 8

Cheddar in Somerset is famous for its cheese but it's also a prime strawberry-growing area, with strawberry fields stretching along the lower slopes of the Mendips. The strawberries were so popular in Victorian times that the Cheddar Valley railway line became known as the Strawberry Line in honour of its precious cargo.

To enjoy these shortcakes at their best, use ripe home-grown strawberries. If you can't find ready-ground pistachios, you can grind the nuts in a small food processor or coffee grinder.

SHORTBREAD
275g plain flour
90g icing sugar
A pinch of salt
150g unsalted butter, diced
1 medium egg
1 tbsp Amaretto liqueur
  (or brandy)
75g ground pistachio nuts

TO ASSEMBLE
200ml double cream
100ml good-quality ready-
  made custard
250g strawberries
Icing sugar, for dusting

EQUIPMENT
An 8.5cm pastry cutter
Piping bag and star nozzle

STEP PHOTOGRAPHS
OVERLEAF

1. To make the shortbread, combine the flour, icing sugar and salt in a bowl and make a well in the centre. Add the butter, egg, liqueur and pistachios. Work the ingredients into the flour with your fingertips to form a smooth dough. Shape into a ball, wrap in cling film and chill for at least 30 minutes.

2. Line 2 baking trays with baking parchment. On a lightly floured surface, roll out the dough to a 5–6mm thickness. Using an 8.5cm cutter, stamp out 16 rounds and place them on the prepared baking trays, re-rolling the trimmings to cut more as necessary. Chill for 15 minutes; this helps to stop the biscuits spreading in the oven. Heat the oven to 170°C/Gas 3.

3. Bake for 12–15 minutes, until the shortbreads are very lightly coloured. Leave them on the baking trays for a few minutes to cool slightly and firm up, then transfer to a wire rack and leave to cool completely.

4. For the filling, whip the cream until fairly stiff, then fold in the custard. Cover and place in the fridge until ready to assemble.

5. Set aside 8 strawberries for decoration; hull the rest and cut into bite-sized pieces. Place the cream mixture in a piping bag fitted with a star nozzle. Arrange the strawberry pieces on half of the biscuits and pipe small stars of cream in between them. Gently place the remaining biscuits on top to sandwich them.

6. Dust the tops of the shortcakes with plenty of icing sugar and decorate with the reserved strawberries, halved.

Working the shortbread mix with the fingertips to form a smooth, homogeneous dough.

Stamping out shortbread rounds, using an 8.5cm pastry cutter.

Shaping the dough into a ball, ready to wrap in cling film and chill before rolling out.

Whipping the cream for the filling until fairly stiff, before folding in the custard.

Piping cream stars in between the strawberry pieces on the baked shortbread bases before sandwiching together with the plain biscuits.

I reckon there could be almost as many recipes for apple cake as there are apple varieties. All apple-growing counties have their own version, with the Dorset apple cake being arguably the easiest and most delicious of all. Cooking apples give a lovely moist cake, while eating apples provide sweetness. I like to combine the two, particularly as the eaters keep their shape and give the cake texture. Some recipes recommend spreading butter on top of the cake while it is hot – even nicer, I think, to serve it with clotted cream.

200g plain flour
1 tsp baking powder
½ tsp ground cinnamon
100g unsalted butter, diced
100g caster sugar
2 eating apples, peeled, cored and thinly sliced
1 small cooking apple, peeled cored and thinly sliced
2 large eggs
60ml milk
1 tbsp demerara sugar

EQUIPMENT
A deep 20cm square cake tin (or a 22cm round tin)

1. Heat the oven to 180°C/Gas 4. Grease a deep 20cm square cake tin (or a 22cm round cake tin) and line the base and sides with baking parchment.

2. Mix the flour, baking powder and cinnamon in a large bowl. Add the butter and rub it in with your fingertips until the mixture resembles fine breadcrumbs.

3. Stir in the sugar, followed by the sliced apples. Lightly beat the eggs with the milk, add to the rubbed-in mixture and stir until well combined.

4. Transfer the mixture to the prepared cake tin. Gently level the surface and sprinkle evenly with the demerara sugar. Bake for 40–50 minutes, until the cake has a golden crust and a skewer inserted in the centre comes out clean.

5. Leave the cake to cool slightly, or completely, in the tin before cutting into squares to serve.

SEED CAKE

MAKES A 20CM CAKE

Caraway seeds are a taste we've pretty much lost now, but seed cakes were a teatime staple in Victorian times. It is thought that they might have been the forerunner of the Bath bun, which dates back to the 18th century. Bath was the cool place to be for wealthy Georgians. They would indulge themselves, then go and bathe in the healing waters. This is a moist, flavoursome cake that keeps well. If you're not keen on caraway, try it with poppy seeds instead.

1. Heat the oven to 180°C/Gas 4. Grease a deep 20cm springform cake tin.

2. Using a handheld electric whisk, beat the butter and sugar together in a bowl until pale and fluffy. Beat in the eggs one at a time.

3. Sift the flour and baking powder into a bowl and mix in the nutmeg, lemon zest and caraway seeds. Fold the flour mix into the whisked mixture, using a spatula or large metal spoon, until evenly combined.

4. Fold in the brandy, then check the consistency of the mixture; it should be soft enough to drop off the spoon when lightly shaken. If it is too dry, add a little milk.

5. Transfer the mixture to the prepared cake tin and bake for 45–50 minutes, until a skewer inserted in the centre of the cake comes out clean. Leave to cool in the tin for 15 minutes before turning out onto a wire rack to cool completely.

200g unsalted butter, softened
200g caster sugar
4 large eggs
200g plain flour
½ tsp baking powder
1 tsp freshly grated nutmeg
Grated zest of 1 lemon
1 tbsp caraway seeds
2 tbsp brandy
A splash of milk, if needed

EQUIPMENT

A deep 20cm springform cake tin

STEP PHOTOGRAPHS OVERLEAF

Whisking the butter and sugar together, using a handheld electric whisk, until pale and fluffy.

Folding the flour mix into the whisked mixture, using a spatula, to avoid knocking out the air that has been incorporated during whisking.

Adding the eggs to the mixture, one at a time, whisking until each egg is just incorporated before adding the next.

Transferring the mixture to the prepared springform cake tin ready for baking.

Checking that the cake is cooked by inserting a skewer into the centre – the skewer should be clean when you take it out.

HEVVA CAKE

MAKES A LARGE SLAB CAKE

Hevva means heavy and this Cornish slab cake is just that – but in a good way. It's hearty, fruity and really satisfying. The criss-cross pattern on top is said to represent fishing nets. Fishermen's wives would spot the boats coming in and whip up this cake quickly – often cooking it on a griddle – so it was ready when their men walked in the door. Traditionally hevva cake uses just lard but I have included some butter for a richer flavour. It is best eaten fresh.

1. Heat the oven to 190°C/Gas 5. Grease a 26 x 20cm baking tin and line it with baking parchment.

2. Mix the flour and salt in a large bowl, add the lard and butter and rub in with your fingertips until the mixture resembles fine breadcrumbs.

3. Stir in the sugar and currants, followed by the egg. Gradually mix in enough milk to bring the mixture together and form a soft dough.

4. Press the dough into the prepared tin and score the top with a diamond pattern. Bake for 30 minutes, until pale golden brown. Leave to cool in the tin before cutting into pieces.

300g plain flour
1 tsp salt
100g lard, diced
100g unsalted butter, diced
100g caster sugar
200g currants
1 large egg, lightly beaten
40–50ml milk

EQUIPMENT

A 26 x 20cm baking tin (or tin with similar dimensions)

CORNISH FAIRINGS

Fairings were little treats sold at fairs throughout the West Country. The Cornish fairing is a crisp ginger biscuit with a distinctive crackled top, produced by adding bicarbonate of soda to the mix. They are so quick to prepare that you can be taking them out of the oven less than half an hour after starting to make them.

200g plain flour
½ tsp salt
1½ tsp baking powder
1½ tsp bicarbonate of soda
1 tsp ground ginger
1 tsp ground cinnamon
100g unsalted butter, diced
100g caster sugar
4 tbsp golden syrup
1 tbsp milk

1. Heat the oven to 180°C/Gas 4. Line 2 baking trays with baking parchment.

2. Mix the flour, salt, baking powder, bicarbonate of soda and spices together in a large bowl. Add the butter and rub in with your fingertips until the mixture resembles fine breadcrumbs. Stir in the sugar.

3. Mix the golden syrup with the milk until dissolved, stir it into the mixture, then bring everything together with your hands to make a dough.

4. Break off small pieces of dough and roll them into small balls. Space them out evenly on the lined baking trays, allowing room for the biscuits to spread during cooking.

5. Bake for about 10 minutes, keeping a close eye on the biscuits as they can darken very quickly towards the end of cooking. They should be an amber colour when done.

6. Leave the biscuits to cool on the baking trays for a few minutes, then transfer to a wire rack to cool completely.

— THE —
SOUTH &
SOUTHEAST

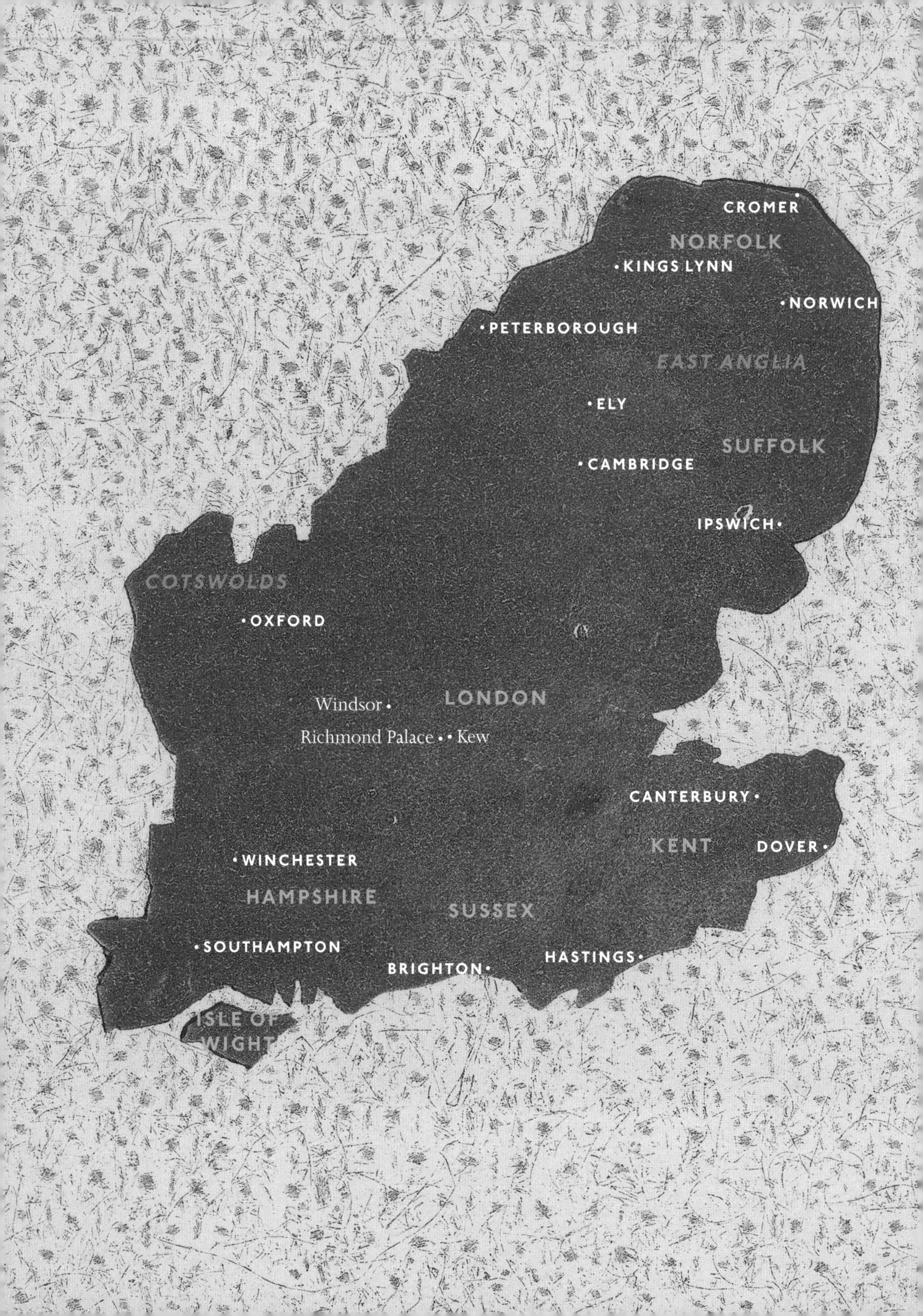
CROMER
NORFOLK
KINGS LYNN
NORWICH
PETERBOROUGH
EAST ANGLIA
ELY
SUFFOLK
CAMBRIDGE
IPSWICH
COTSWOLDS
OXFORD
Windsor
LONDON
Richmond Palace
Kew
CANTERBURY
KENT
DOVER
WINCHESTER
HAMPSHIRE
SUSSEX
SOUTHAMPTON
BRIGHTON
HASTINGS
ISLE OF WIGHT

For anyone brought up in the hilly regions of the British Isles, the flatlands of East Anglia can seem like alien territory. Farmland stretches out uninterrupted for miles, much of it former marshes that have been drained. But it is this terrain that has brought the area prosperity – fertile land for growing wheat and barley, vegetables such as potatoes, peas and celery, plus apples and soft fruit. Windmills are still a familiar sight in the area, a reminder of how much grain was produced here in the past.

With a ready supply of good wheat, baking was always going to be an important culinary tradition in this part of the country. The fat of choice for pastries and cakes was originally lard, as many rural households kept a pig, while suet was used to make steamed puddings such as the Norfolk plough pudding on page 68 and, one of the southern counties' crowning glories, Sussex pond pudding (page 74).

Kent and Sussex still have some claim to their reputation as the Garden of England – though they're just as likely to grow grapes for wine as fruit for the table these days. The brief season for Kentish cherries is eagerly awaited, while some of our finest apple varieties originate from this area, including Cox's Orange Pippin and Bramley. It is no coincidence that the National Fruit Collections – home to around 4,000 varieties of fruit – are to be found in Kent.

Some of the least familiar recipes appear in this chapter. Although most of us know and love Eton mess (page 85), Kentish huffkins (page 89) and Sussex churdles (page 71) are another matter entirely. Their picturesque names are a reminder of past times, and a more rural, unhurried way of life. It has been exciting to discover these and other recipes, such as the Isle of Wight doughnuts (page 90) that are barely to be found on the island any more, and heavies (page 100), a way of using up little scraps of dough to make treats for children.

It's not all hay wains and rural idylls, though. The South of England has a royal past as well as a rustic one, as Maids of Honour (page 99), supposedly a favourite of Henry VIII, and Osborne pudding (page 80), from Queen Victoria's residence on the Isle of Wight, remind us.

NORFOLK PLOUGH PUDDING

SUET PASTRY

285g self-raising flour
1 tsp baking powder
125g suet
2 tsp finely chopped sage
About 200ml water
Salt and pepper

FILLING

400g good-quality sausagemeat
200g pancetta, diced
1 onion, diced
2 tsp finely chopped thyme
1 tsp dark muscovado sugar

EQUIPMENT

A 1.2 litre pudding basin

Pork crops up a lot in Norfolk recipes. It used to be common for families to keep a pig, to be killed in autumn then potted, salted, and made into pies and black puddings. Traditionally this one was served on Plough Monday, the first Monday after Twelfth Night. A plough would be blessed ceremoniously before work began again.

1. Generously butter a 1.2 litre pudding basin and line the base with a disc of baking parchment.

2. For the pastry, mix the flour, baking powder, suet, sage and some salt and pepper together. Gradually stir in enough water to make a soft, slightly sticky dough. Cut off a third and roll out on a floured surface to a circle slightly larger than the top of the basin. Invert the basin onto it and cut round it to form a lid; set aside. Briefly knead the offcuts into the larger piece of dough. Roll out to a circle, 30cm in diameter, and use to line the pudding basin, leaving the excess overhanging the edge.

3. Roll out the sausagemeat between 2 sheets of cling film to a circle just large enough to line the pudding. Lift it into the basin and press it onto the pastry to line. Mix the remaining filling ingredients together, season with pepper and spoon into the basin. Dampen the pastry edges with water, position the pastry lid on top and press the edges to seal. Trim away excess pastry.

4. Following the instructions on page 74 (see step 4), make a cover for the basin using baking parchment and foil. Position and secure with string, tying this to form a handle.

5. Stand the pudding basin in a large steamer, cover and steam for 2½–3 hours, topping up the boiling water as necessary so it doesn't boil dry. (Or use a large saucepan containing enough boiling water to come halfway up the side of the basin.)

6. Lift out the pudding, remove the cover and rest for 5 minutes. Use a knife to release the sides of the pudding from the basin. Put a large plate over the pudding and invert both together to turn out the pudding. Serve with mashed potatoes and gravy.

SUSSEX CHURDLES

MAKES 4

These delicious little savoury pies were a staple for agricultural workers to take with them while working the land. Made with a hot-water crust pastry, like pork pies, they have a rustic, freeform shape. Hot-water crust is great for portable food and was often used for workers' meals. The upper classes were more likely to have their pies encased in a refined shortcrust pastry.

HOT-WATER PASTRY

275g plain flour
100g strong white bread flour
50g unsalted butter, diced
135ml water
A pinch of salt
70g lard, diced
1 egg, lightly beaten, to glaze

FILLING

25g butter
1 onion, finely chopped
200g streaky bacon, chopped
200g lamb's liver, cut into
  bite-sized pieces
1 tbsp chopped sage
1 eating apple, peeled, cored
  and sliced
25g white breadcrumbs
25g strong Cheddar cheese,
  grated
Salt and pepper

EQUIPMENT

An 18cm plate (to use as a guide)

STEP PHOTOGRAPHS
OVERLEAF

1. Start by making the filling. Melt the butter in a wide pan, add the onion and cook gently until soft but not coloured. Add the bacon, raise the heat a little, and cook until it starts to crisp around the edges. Stir in the liver and cook until it is just sealed. Remove from the heat, stir in the sage and apple and season with salt and a little pepper. Leave to cool.

2. To make the pastry, combine the flours in a bowl, add the butter and rub in lightly with your fingertips. Heat the water, salt and lard in a saucepan until the lard has melted and the mixture has just come to the boil. Pour the mixture into the flour and stir quickly with a wooden spoon until combined. Turn the dough out onto a lightly floured surface and knead briefly until smooth.

3. Working as quickly as you can (the pastry becomes crumbly as it cools), divide the pastry into 4 pieces. Roll out each one and cut out an 18cm circle, using a plate as a guide.

4. Divide the cooled filling between the pastry circles, spooning it into a mound in the centre. Gather the pastry up around the filling, pinching little pleats around the edge to hold the filling in place, leaving the top open. Place on a tray in the fridge to firm up for a few hours, or even overnight.

5. Heat the oven to 200°C/Gas 6. Line a baking tray with baking parchment and transfer the pastries to it. Mix the breadcrumbs and cheese together and sprinkle them over the filling. Brush the pastry with beaten egg and bake for 20–25 minutes, until the pastry is crisp and golden and the topping is crunchy.

Quickly stirring the hot water and melted lard mix into the rubbed-in mixture to make the hot-water pastry.

Briefly kneading the pastry on a lightly floured surface until smooth.

Cutting the hot-water pastry into 4 equal pieces.

Rolling out a portion of the pastry to a round, large enough to trim to a neat 18cm circle.

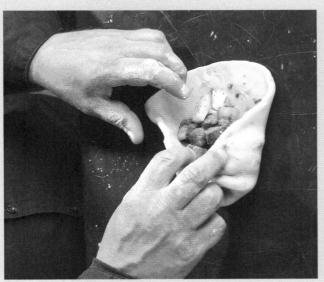

Gathering the edges of the pastry up around the filling to contain it.

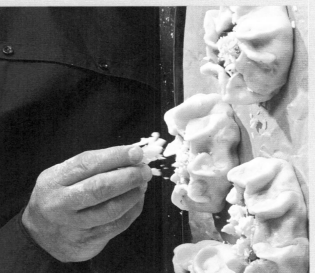

Sprinkling the cheese and breadcrumb mix on top of the filling before baking.

Spooning the cooled savoury filling into the centre of the pastry circle.

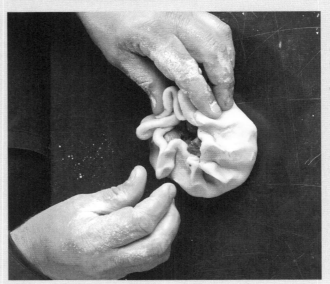

Pinching the pastry edges together to form little pleats, leaving the top of the parcel open.

There's nothing quite like this pudding. A whole lemon is steamed inside a suet crust with butter and brown sugar for several hours. As you cut into the pud, the juice of the lemon floods out with the butter and sugar to make a tangy sauce. Serve with thick cream.

200g self-raising flour
20g caster sugar
125g suet
2 large lemons
150–175ml whole milk
150g light soft brown sugar
150g unsalted butter, cut into
1–2cm cubes

EQUIPMENT
A 1.2 litre pudding basin

**STEP PHOTOGRAPHS
OVERLEAF**

1. Butter a 1.2 litre pudding basin. Put the flour, sugar and suet in a bowl and grate in the zest from 1 lemon. Gradually stir in enough milk to form a soft, slightly sticky dough.

2. Take a third of the pastry and roll it out on a floured surface to a circle slightly bigger than the basin. Invert the basin onto the pastry and cut around it to form a lid. Briefly knead the offcuts into the larger piece of dough and then roll it out to a circle, roughly 30cm in diameter. Use to line the pudding basin.

3. Spoon the brown sugar into the pastry-lined basin. Pierce the non-zested lemon all over with a skewer and sit it on top of the sugar. Surround with the diced butter. Dampen the edges of the pastry with milk or water and position the pastry lid on top. Trim off the excess pastry and press the edges together to seal.

4. Place a piece of baking parchment on a sheet of foil and make a large pleat in the middle, folding both sheets together (this allows the pudding to expand as it cooks). Place, foil-side up, over the basin and secure with string, looping the end over the top of the pudding and tying it to form a handle that will make it easier to lift the pudding in and out of the saucepan.

5. Stand the pudding basin in a large steamer, cover and steam for 3 hours, topping up the boiling water if necessary so it doesn't boil dry. (Or use a large saucepan containing enough boiling water to come halfway up the side of the basin.)

6. Lift the basin from the pan, take off the cover and release the sides of the pudding with a knife. Invert a deep plate over the basin and turn both together to unmould the pudding. Serve at once, cutting carefully as the juices will flood out. Give each person a small piece of the cooked lemon as you serve.

Rolling out the two-thirds portion of pastry into a large circle, about 30cm in diameter, to line the pudding basin.

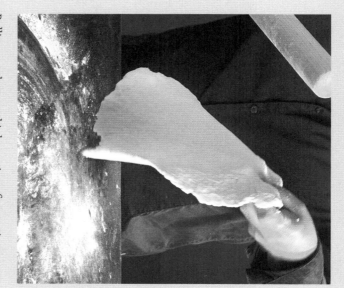

Folding the pastry to make it easier to lower into the pudding basin.

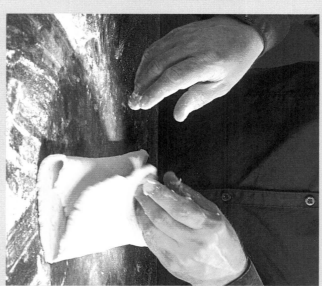

Unfolding the pastry and pressing it gently to the sides of the basin to line it, leaving the excess overhanging; make sure that there are no cracks.

Spreading the brown sugar in the bottom of the pastry-lined basin and making a slight hollow in the middle for the whole lemon.

Adding the diced butter cubes around the whole lemon in the middle.

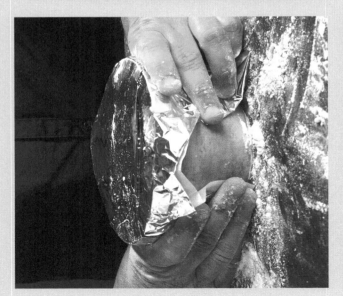

Pressing the edges of the pastry lid to the rim of the pastry lining the basin to seal the pudding.

Running a knife around the sides of the steamed pudding to release it from the basin.

Positioning the pleated foil and parchment cover over the top of the pudding and pressing it under the rim of the basin, ready to secure with string.

POOR KNIGHTS OF WINDSOR

SERVES 4

Supposedly named after medieval knights who could afford to eat only humble food after being bankrupted by wars with France, this is very similar to eggy bread, or *pain perdu*. The difference is that the egg and milk for dipping the bread are kept apart and there is an added kick from sherry. I love the contrast in flavours here: the sweetness of the bread, the richness of the egg and the sharpness of the raspberries. Serve with ice cream or thick cream.

4 slices of stale white bread,
    about 1cm thick
100ml sweet sherry
150ml milk
4 egg yolks
2 tbsp caster sugar
50g unsalted butter

RASPBERRY SAUCE
250g raspberries
3 tbsp icing sugar
Juice of ½ lemon

1. To make the sauce, put the raspberries, icing sugar and lemon juice in a pan and cook gently for a few minutes, until the raspberries begin to soften but still hold their shape. Cover and remove from the heat.

2. Cut the crusts off the bread, if preferred. Put the sherry and milk into separate shallow bowls, large enough to hold a slice of bread. In a third shallow bowl, beat the egg yolks with the sugar to combine.

3. Melt the butter in a large frying pan over a low-medium heat. Dip each slice of bread in the sherry, then the milk and finally into the egg yolk mixture, before adding it straight to the pan. Fry for 2–3 minutes per side, until golden brown. (Alternatively, you can use a small frying pan and cook the bread slices one at a time.)

4. Transfer the slices of bread to serving plates, cut them into fingers or triangles if you like, and serve straight away with the raspberry sauce.

OSBORNE PUDDING

SERVES 6

Supposedly a favourite of Queen Victoria, who often stayed at Osborne House on the Isle of Wight, this variation on bread and butter pudding is made with brown bread and marmalade. Preferring nursery food to more sophisticated dining, the queen had a famously sweet tooth.

50g unsalted butter, softened

6–8 slices of thick-cut brown bread

2 tbsp marmalade

175ml whole milk

325ml double cream

1 vanilla pod

6 egg yolks

50g caster sugar

75g raisins

Grated zest of 1 orange

1 tbsp demerara sugar

EQUIPMENT

A 23 x 18cm ovenproof dish (or dish with similar dimensions)

STEP PHOTOGRAPHS
OVERLEAF

1. Lightly grease an ovenproof dish, about 23 x 18cm, with butter. Cut the crusts off the bread. Butter the bread slices generously with the remaining butter, then spread with the marmalade and cut each slice in half on the diagonal.

2. Put the milk and cream in a saucepan. Slit the vanilla pod open lengthwise and scrape out the seeds, then add the seeds and pod to the pan. Heat to just below boiling.

3. Meanwhile, whisk the egg yolks and caster sugar together in a large bowl or jug. Gradually pour on the hot cream mixture, whisking until smooth. Remove the vanilla pod.

4. Pour a little custard over the base of the buttered ovenproof dish and sprinkle over half the raisins.

5. Arrange the bread in the dish in overlapping slices, with the points upward. Sprinkle the orange zest and the rest of the raisins over the bread and pour on the remaining custard. Leave to stand for 30 minutes so the bread can absorb some of the custard. Heat the oven to 170°C/Gas 3.

6. Sprinkle the demerara sugar over the pudding and bake for about 30 minutes, until the custard has just set. Leave to stand for 10–15 minutes, then serve with double cream or ice cream.

Spreading the buttered slices of bread with the marmalade.

Pouring the hot vanilla-infused cream and milk mixture onto the egg and sugar mix and whisking until smooth.

Pouring the rest of the vanilla custard over the bread slices.

Whisking the egg yolks and sugar together in a bowl until evenly combined.

Arranging the bread triangles in the ovenproof dish, on a layer of custard and raisins.

ETON MESS

SERVES 6–8

This must have come about as a result of an accident. Why else would you make a perfectly good meringue and smash it up? It has to be said, the result is sublime. In this version, I've unmessed the pud by making tiny individual meringues that don't need to be broken up. It retains all the character of the original, but adds charm. You will have more meringues than you need but it's not practical to make less mixture. Keep the rest in an airtight tin to eat when you fancy.

1. Heat the oven to 120°C/Gas ½. Line 2 baking sheets with baking parchment.

2. To make the meringues, whisk the egg whites until stiff, then add the sugar a spoonful at a time, whisking well after each addition. Once all the sugar has been incorporated, the meringue should be thick and glossy.

3. Transfer half the meringue to a separate bowl and fold in the freeze-dried strawberry pieces. Fold a tiny amount of red food colouring into the remaining meringue to give a pink shade.

4. Put the meringue mixtures into separate piping bags, each fitted with a 1cm plain nozzle. Pipe small blobs of meringue, about 1cm in diameter, onto the prepared baking sheets.

5. Bake in the oven for 1–1¼ hours, until the meringues are crisp and can be peeled easily off the baking parchment. Turn off the oven but leave the meringues inside, with the door slightly open, to cool completely.

6. Purée half the strawberries with 1 tbsp of the icing sugar. Halve or quarter the rest and mix with a good splash of Cointreau.

7. Put the cream in a bowl, add the remaining icing sugar and whisk to soft peaks.

8. To serve, layer the strawberries, whipped cream, meringues and strawberry purée in wide glasses.

MERINGUES

2 egg whites
115g caster sugar
2g freeze-dried strawberry
  pieces
A little red food colouring

TO ASSEMBLE

500g strawberries
3 tbsp icing sugar
A splash of Cointreau
400ml double cream

EQUIPMENT

2 piping bags and 1cm plain
  nozzles

NORFOLK KNOBS

MAKES 24

150g strong white bread flour
75g plain flour
½ tsp salt
1 tsp instant yeast
40g lard, diced and softened
About 150ml water

These are similar to the better known Dorset knobs, which are still made commercially. Also known as hollow cakes, these crisp little rolls have a texture like rusks. After the initial baking, they are dried out in a very low oven until crisp. Serve split open and spread with butter and jam, or with cheese or pâté.

1. Put the flours in a large bowl and add the salt on one side, the yeast on the other. Add the lard and three-quarters of the water, then turn the mixture round with the fingers of one hand. Add the remaining water a little at a time, continuing to mix until you have taken in all the flour from the side of the bowl and the dough is soft and slightly sticky.

2. Tip the dough onto a lightly floured work surface and knead for at least 5 minutes to a smooth, soft dough. (It will be quite sticky and difficult to work at first, so persevere.) Lightly oil the bowl, return the dough to it and cover with cling film. Leave to rise for at least an hour, until doubled in size.

3. Line 1 or 2 large baking tray(s) with baking parchment. Scrape the dough out onto a lightly floured surface and fold it inwards repeatedly until all the air is knocked out and it is smooth.

4. Roll out the dough to a 1cm thick rectangle, about 30 x 18cm. Fold the top down to the centre, then fold the bottom up to meet it. Turn the dough over and roll out to 1cm thick again, then prick all over with a fork.

5. Cut the dough into 24 small squares. Roll into balls and place on the lined tray(s). Put each tray into a clean plastic bag and leave to prove for 1 hour. Heat the oven to 200°C/Gas 6.

6. Bake for 12–15 minutes until the rolls are golden brown and sound hollow when tapped underneath. Leave them to cool on a wire rack. Lower the oven setting to 120°C/Gas ½.

7. Return the knobs to the oven for 1¾ hours to dry out. Leave to cool completely before eating.

KENTISH HUFFKINS

MAKES 8

500g strong white bread flour
1 tsp salt
2 tsp sugar
7g sachet instant yeast
50g unsalted butter, diced
    and softened
150ml milk
150ml water

These large, flat bread rolls are made from a fairly standard dough; it's the dimple in the middle that makes them huffkins. I've heard that a cobnut used to be placed in the centre – a nice Kentish touch. I enjoy them with butter and cherry jam but they're also very good filled with ham or cheese.

1. Put the flour in a large bowl. Add the salt and sugar on one side, the yeast on the other. Add the butter, milk and three-quarters of the water, then turn the mixture round with the fingers of one hand. Add the remaining water a little at a time, continuing to mix until all the flour is taken in and the dough is soft and slightly sticky; you might not need all the water.

2. Coat the work surface with a little oil to prevent the dough sticking. Turn out the dough and knead for at least 5 minutes, until it is smooth and no longer sticky. Lightly oil the bowl, return the dough to it and cover with cling film. Leave to rise for at least an hour, until doubled in size.

3. Line 2 baking trays with baking parchment. Scrape the dough out onto a lightly floured surface and fold it inwards repeatedly until all the air is knocked out and the dough is smooth. Divide into 8 pieces.

4. Roll each piece into a ball by placing it into a cage formed by your hand on the work surface and moving your hand in a circular motion, rotating the ball rapidly. Flatten the top by pressing with your hand.

5. Put the balls of dough on the prepared baking trays, spacing them slightly apart. Place each tray in a clean plastic bag and leave to prove for about 40 minutes, until the huffkins have doubled in size. Heat the oven to 220°C/Gas 7.

6. Just before baking, dust the huffkins with flour and make an indentation in the centre of each with your floured thumb. Bake for 15 minutes, until golden brown. Immediately wrap the rolls in a clean tea towel, to achieve their characteristic soft crust.

The Isle of Wight is thought to be the first place to sell doughnuts in Britain, possibly developed from the Dutch version, *oliebollen*. These doughnuts are filled with dried fruit and candied peel rather than jam, giving them a festive taste.

300g strong white bread flour

1 tsp ground nutmeg

½ tsp salt

50g caster sugar, plus extra for coating

7g sachet instant yeast

50g unsalted butter, diced and softened

150–175ml milk

2 tbsp currants

1 tbsp mixed candied peel

¼ tsp ground cinnamon

Vegetable oil for deep-frying

STEP PHOTOGRAPHS OVERLEAF

1. Put the flour and nutmeg in a large bowl and add the salt and sugar on one side, the yeast on the other. Add the butter and 120ml of the milk then turn the mixture with the fingers of one hand. Add the remaining milk a little at a time, mixing until you have taken in all the flour and the dough is soft and slightly sticky; you might not need all the milk.

2. Turn the dough out onto a lightly floured surface and knead for at least 5 minutes, until smooth and no longer sticky. Lightly oil the bowl, return the dough to it and cover with cling film. Leave to rise for at least an hour, until doubled in size.

3. Line 2 baking trays with baking parchment. Scrape the dough out onto a lightly floured surface and fold inwards repeatedly until all the air is knocked out and the dough is smooth. Divide into 12 pieces and roll each into a ball (as shown overleaf).

4. Mix the currants, peel and cinnamon together. Make a small hole in each ball and push in a little of the filling. Pull the dough round the filling to seal it in and roll again if necessary to reshape. Put the balls of dough on the prepared trays, spacing them slightly apart. Place each tray in a clean plastic bag and leave to prove for about 45 minutes, until doubled in size.

5. Heat the oil in a deep-fat fryer or deep saucepan to 180°C. If the filling has become exposed, gently re-seal the doughnuts. Fry them in the hot oil, in 3 or 4 batches, for 6–8 minutes, until cooked through, turning them with a slotted spoon halfway through so they colour evenly.

6. Remove the doughnuts from the pan with a slotted spoon and drain on kitchen paper. Roll them in caster sugar to coat liberally. Leave to cool for a few minutes before serving.

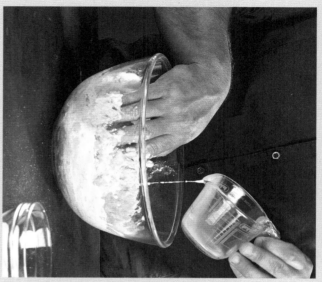

Turning the mixture with the fingers of one hand to incorporate as much of the remaining milk as is needed to obtain a soft, slightly sticky dough.

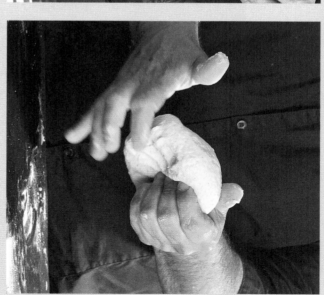

Kneading the dough until it is smooth and no longer sticky; this will take at least 5 minutes.

Folding the risen dough inwards and pressing down on it to knock out the air.

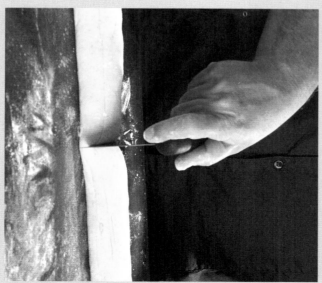

Dividing the dough into 12 pieces, by cutting it first in half, then into quarters, then cutting each piece into 3.

Combining the currants, candied peel and spice for the filling, ready to insert into the shaped balls of dough.

Deep-frying the doughnuts in batches, to avoid overcrowding the pan.

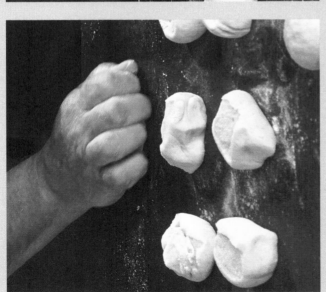

Forming a cage over one piece of dough and moving the hand in a circular motion, to rotate the dough rapidly and shape it into a neat ball.

Pulling the dough around the filling to enclose it completely and pressing the edges of the dough together to seal.

CIDER CAKE

MAKES AN 18CM CAKE

100g unsalted butter
100g light soft brown sugar
2 large eggs
225g plain flour
1 tsp bicarbonate of soda
1 tsp ground cinnamon
150ml dry cider
Icing sugar, for dusting

EQUIPMENT

A deep 18cm round cake tin

This is a light, plain cake, with a hint of apple flavour. Cider cakes are teatime favourites in cider-producing areas and many recipes use bicarbonate of soda as the raising agent. To activate it, you need an acidic ingredient and dry English cider does the job perfectly.

1. Heat the oven to 180°C/Gas 4. Grease a deep 18cm round cake tin and line the base with baking parchment.

2. Beat the butter and sugar together with a handheld electric whisk until pale and fluffy, then beat in the eggs one at a time. Sift the flour, bicarbonate of soda and cinnamon together.

3. Fold about a third of the flour mix into the whisked mixture, then fold in half of the cider, with a large metal spoon or spatula. Fold in another third of the flour, then the rest of the cider. Finally fold in the remaining flour until evenly combined.

4. Transfer the mixture to the prepared cake tin and gently level the surface. Bake for 30–40 minutes, until a skewer inserted in the centre comes out clean.

5. Leave the cake to cool in the tin for 20 minutes, then turn out onto a wire rack and set aside to cool completely. Dust with icing sugar to serve.

KENTISH CHERRY CAKE

MAKES A 20CM CAKE

We have Henry VIII to thank for Kentish cherries. He ordered the fruit trees to be planted in the county, which has been associated with them ever since — though only around a tenth of the original 5,000 hectares of cherry orchards remain.

If you're lucky enough to be able to get cherries from Kent, buy plenty, so you can enjoy them from the punnet and have some left over to make this cake. It's great served warm with ice cream, or you can top it with a citrus glacé icing made with 200g icing sugar and enough lemon or orange juice to give a fairly thick icing.

250g cherries
100g unsalted butter, softened
100g caster sugar
2 medium eggs
100g plain flour
¼ tsp baking powder
50g ground almonds
1 tbsp milk
icing sugar, for dusting

EQUIPMENT

A shallow 20cm round cake tin

1. Heat the oven to 180°C/Gas 4. Grease a shallow 20cm round cake tin (a sandwich tin is fine to use) and line the base with baking parchment.

2. Cut the cherries in half and remove the stones. Pat the cherries dry with kitchen paper and leave to one side.

3. Put the butter and sugar in a bowl and beat together until pale and fluffy. Beat in the eggs one at a time.

4. Sift the flour and baking powder over the mixture and fold in with a large metal spoon or spatula. Toss three-quarters of the cherries with the ground almonds, then fold them gently into the cake mixture. Stir in the milk.

5. Transfer the mixture to the prepared cake tin and gently smooth the surface. Scatter the remaining cherries over the top and press them lightly into the mixture. Bake for 25–30 minutes, until the cake is risen and golden, and a skewer inserted in the centre comes out clean.

6. Leave the cake in the tin for 10 minutes, then transfer to a wire rack to cool. Dust with icing sugar before serving.

MAIDS OF HONOUR

MAKES 12

These little sweet cheese tarts are something of a mystery. They are thought to have been developed by a cook at Richmond Palace and much enjoyed by Henry VIII, although a slightly different story has it that the king found Anne Boleyn and her maids eating them and named them on the spot. A teashop in Kew, dating right back to the 18th century, claims to have the original recipe, which is kept a close secret. There are plenty of variations, though, most of them relying on curd cheese, ground almonds and eggs. I've opted for an orange-flavoured version here. You could use rosewater instead.

250g good-quality ready-made all-butter puff pastry

FILLING

35g unsalted butter, softened
50g caster sugar
50g curd cheese
2 large eggs
50g ground almonds
1 tsp orange flower water
Grated zest of 1 orange

TO FINISH

Icing sugar, for dusting

EQUIPMENT

A 12-hole bun tray
A 9cm pastry cutter

1. Heat the oven to 180°C/Gas 4. Roll out the pastry on a lightly floured surface to a 2–3mm thickness. Using a 9cm cutter, cut out 12 circles and use them to line a bun tray (the kind you would use for fairy cakes, not a deep muffin tray).

2. For the filling, beat the butter, sugar and curd cheese together in a bowl until smooth. Beat in the eggs one at a time, then stir in the ground almonds, orange flower water and orange zest. Spoon the filling into the pastry cases.

3. Bake for 20–25 minutes, until the pastry is crisp and golden and the filling is well risen and just set.

4. Leave the tarts to cool in the tray for 5 minutes, then carefully release and place on a wire rack to cool. Dust with icing sugar before serving. They are nicest eaten fresh.

CHOCOLATE HEAVIES

MAKES 20

Plum heavies, from Sussex, were popular biscuits with children in Victorian times. Leftover pastry scraps had currants or raisins kneaded into them before being cut into biscuits — the lack of a raising agent resulted in the name heavies. Here I'm using self-raising flour for a lighter result and dark chocolate chips to replace the currants — something Victorian children almost certainly missed out on. You could, of course, stick to the spirit of the recipe and use currants or whatever you have to hand.

225g self-raising flour

¼ tsp salt

50g unsalted butter, diced

50g lard, diced

75g caster sugar

75g dark chocolate chips

About 40ml milk

1 egg, lightly beaten, to glaze

EQUIPMENT

A 6.5cm pastry cutter

1. Mix the flour and salt in a bowl, add the butter and lard and rub them in with your fingertips until the mixture resembles fine breadcrumbs.

2. Stir in the sugar and chocolate chips, then add enough milk to bring the mixture together into a dough. Wrap in cling film and rest in the fridge for 20 minutes.

3. Heat the oven to 190°C/Gas 5. Line 2 baking trays with baking parchment.

4. On a lightly floured surface, roll out the dough to a 5mm thickness. Using a 6.5cm cutter, stamp out circles and place them on the lined baking trays. Press the offcuts together, re-roll them and cut out more biscuits.

5. Brush with beaten egg and bake for about 10 minutes, until the biscuits are golden brown. Leave on the baking trays for a few minutes, then transfer to a wire rack to cool. These biscuits are best eaten fresh.

THE — MIDLANDS

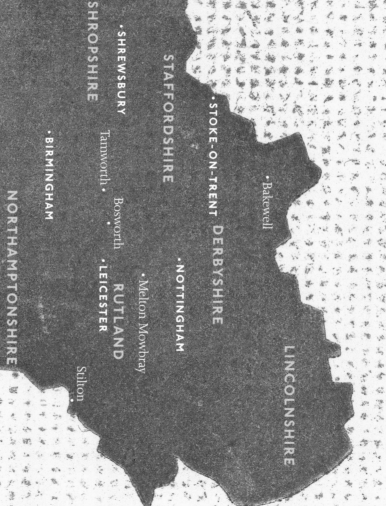

HEREFORDSHIRE

• Hereford

WORCESTER •

SHROPSHIRE

• SHREWSBURY

STAFFORDSHIRE

• STOKE-ON-TRENT

DERBYSHIRE

• Bakewell

• BIRMINGHAM

Tamworth •

Bosworth

NOTTINGHAM •

NORTHAMPTONSHIRE

• STRATFORD-UPON-AVON

• LEICESTER

RUTLAND

• Melton Mowbray

LINCOLNSHIRE

Stilton •

The Midlands is where much of the Industrial Revolution kicked off. It's also home to some of our best-loved foods: Bakewell pudding, pork pies, Staffordshire oatcakes and cheeses such as Stilton, Cheshire and Red Leicester, to name but a few. Much of the region is dairy-farming country – hence the cheeses and dairy-rich puddings – but it is also renowned for its pork, particularly the Tamworth pig. Hereford and Worcester are famous for their orchards, while the Vale of Evesham produces fine asparagus.

With these riches, it is hardly surprising that the area's culinary heritage lives up to its industrial one. The fertile land gave bakers plenty of ingredients to choose from when making pies, puddings and cakes. Local delicacies are strongly rooted in the produce of the area, from the little cheesecakes of Northamptonshire (page 135), filled with fresh curds, to Lincolnshire plum bread (page 129), traditionally made with lard, and Hereford apple dumplings (page 114), an unusual way to turn apples into a feast.

When it comes to savoury pies, the Melton Mowbray pork pie is justly celebrated, but the fidget pies of Shropshire (page 106) deserve a revival too. Filled with gammon, apple and cider, they're a fine example of how ingredients that are produced together taste great together.

One recipe that links farming and industry is the Staffordshire oatcake (page 125). Unique to the region, these large, holey pancakes are made from the oats that used to grow locally, and were eaten by workers in the potteries and mines to sustain them through a long, hard day. Homity pie (page 110), also connected with the Midlands, was a means of nourishing people cheaply and thriftily during wartime.

Conversely, several of the substantial dishes of the region were created not for the workers but to feed the wealthy. Leicestershire, Northamptonshire and the tiny county of Rutland used to have a reputation as the best hunting country in Britain. Melton Hunt cake (page 136) was traditionally enjoyed before the hunt, while afterwards the participants would tuck into a substantial feast of pies and cakes to keep them going till dinnertime, which might have been rounded off with a hearty steamed hunting pudding (page 113).

FIDGET PIES

Fidget pie — sometimes called fitchett pie — was enjoyed by farm workers at harvest time throughout the Midlands, particularly in Shropshire. The cider gives the filling a great flavour lift. I've opted to make individual pies here, the perfect size to hold in the hand.

PASTRY

300g plain flour
A pinch of salt
75g cold unsalted butter, diced
75g cold lard, diced
About 4 tbsp ice-cold water
1 egg, lightly beaten, to glaze

FILLING

1 potato (about 200g)
1 small onion, thinly sliced
275g cooked gammon, diced
1 small cooking apple, peeled, cored and thinly sliced
2 tbsp chopped parsley
1½ tbsp cornflour
100ml dry cider
Salt and pepper

EQUIPMENT

A 12-hole muffin tray
A 7.5cm pastry cutter

STEP PHOTOGRAPHS
OVERLEAF

1. To make the pastry, put the flour and salt into a large bowl, add the butter and lard and rub them in with your fingertips until the mixture resembles fine breadcrumbs. Gradually mix in enough water to form a dough. Knead briefly until smooth; do not overwork it. Wrap in cling film and chill for 30 minutes.

2. Heat the oven to 200°C/Gas 6. Cut off a third of the pastry and set aside for the pie lids. On a lightly floured surface, roll the larger portion into a cylinder. Cut into 12 even slices and roll each into a 10cm circle, about 3mm thick. Use these to line a muffin tray. Roll out the other portion of pastry to a 2mm thickness and use a 7.5cm cutter to cut out 12 lids for the pies.

3. For the filling, peel and thinly slice the potato. Arrange a layer of potato slices in the base of each pie case, cutting them to fit as necessary. Add a layer of onion and season with a little salt and pepper. Divide the gammon between the pastry cases, then add a layer of apple slices and a final layer of potato. Sprinkle the chopped parsley on top.

4. Put the cornflour in a small bowl and slowly stir in the cider, keeping the mixture smooth. Add 2 tsp of this liquid to each pie. Dampen the rim of the pastry with a little water and top each pie with a lid, pressing down well to seal the edges. Make a small slit in the top of each pie and brush with beaten egg.

5. Bake for 30–35 minutes, until the pastry is crisp and golden. Leave to cool in the tin for 10 minutes, then run a knife around the edge of each pie and turn out. Serve hot or cold.

Gently rolling the larger (two-thirds) portion of pastry into an even cylinder.

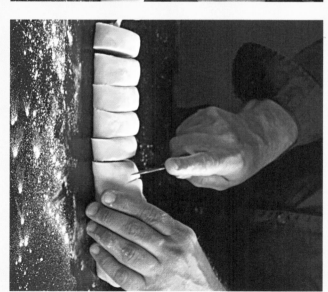

Cutting the pastry into 12 even pieces, for the individual pie cases.

Rolling out one piece of pastry thinly to a 10cm circle, about 3mm thick.

Easing the pastry circle into the muffin tray and pressing it gently into the corners.

Adding 2 tsp of the cider and cornflour mixture to each pie.

Cutting a small slit in the top of each pie using a small, sharp knife, to allow steam to escape during cooking.

Dividing the gammon between the pie cases, placing it on top of the potato and onion layers.

Positioning the pie lids over the filling.

Made with wholemeal pastry and filled with potatoes, onions, leeks and cheese, this tart was originally devised by land girls working on farms during the Second World War. At one point, the cheese ration was a mere ounce (28g) per person per week. My recipe is austerity-free, with Cheddar, Parmesan and a little cream.

1. To make the pastry, put the flours and salt into a bowl, add the butter and rub it in with your fingertips until the mixture resembles fine breadcrumbs, then make a well in the centre. Mix the egg yolk with the water. Stir into the mixture with a round-bladed knife, adding a little more water if it seems too dry. When the dough begins to stick together, gently knead it into a smooth ball. Wrap in cling film and leave to rest in the fridge while you make the filling.

2. For the filling, peel the potatoes and cut into 2cm chunks. Cook in boiling salted water until tender, then drain and leave to cool. Heat the butter and oil in a frying pan, add the onions, leeks and a pinch of salt and cook gently until soft. Stir in the garlic and remove from the heat.

3. Place the potatoes, onions, leeks and garlic in a large bowl. Stir in the Cheddar, parsley, thyme and cream and season well with salt and pepper. Set aside.

4. Heat the oven to 200°C/Gas 6. Put a baking tray inside to heat.

5. On a lightly floured surface, roll out the pastry to about a 3mm thickness. Use it to line a 20cm loose-bottomed tin, about 4cm deep (a sandwich cake tin is ideal) and trim the pastry edges. Spoon the filling into the pastry case. Mix the breadcrumbs with the grated Parmesan and sprinkle evenly over the top.

6. Stand the tin on the hot baking tray and bake the pie for about 40 minutes, until the pastry is cooked through and the topping is crisp and golden brown. Remove from the oven and leave to stand for 5–10 minutes before removing from the tin and serving, or leave to cool. A leafy salad is the ideal complement.

PASTRY

100g plain flour
50g wholemeal flour
¼ tsp salt
75g unsalted butter, diced
1 egg yolk
1 tbsp cold water

FILLING

350g waxy potatoes, such as Charlotte or Ratte
10g butter
1 tbsp sunflower oil
2 onions, sliced
2 leeks, sliced
1 garlic clove, finely chopped
175g mature Cheddar cheese, grated
1 tbsp chopped parsley
1 tbsp thyme leaves
1 tbsp double cream
3 tbsp panko breadcrumbs
1½ tbsp freshly grated Parmesan cheese
Salt and pepper

EQUIPMENT

A deep 20cm loose-bottomed tart tin or sandwich cake tin

LEICESTERSHIRE HUNTING PUDDING

SERVES 4

Typically, this moist, fruity steamed suet pudding would have been served after a day's hunting. Traditionally it was made as one large pudding, but I like to make it in individual moulds. It always feels like a treat to get a little pudding all to yourself.

100g self-raising flour
100g suet
100g light muscovado sugar
½ tsp freshly grated nutmeg
200g sultanas
Grated zest and juice of 1 lemon
1 tbsp brandy
2 large eggs, lightly beaten

EQUIPMENT

4 dariole moulds (175ml capacity)

1. Butter four 175ml dariole moulds or mini pudding basins and line the base of each one with a disc of baking parchment.

2. Place the flour, suet, sugar and nutmeg in a bowl and stir to combine, then stir in the sultanas. Now add the lemon zest and juice, brandy and beaten eggs. Stir gently to combine and make a stiff mixture.

3. Divide the mixture between the prepared moulds. Tap each mould on the work surface to remove any air pockets and level out the mixture.

4. Make a lid for each pudding by placing a small piece of baking parchment over a small piece of foil and pleating them in the middle by folding both sheets together (this allows room for the puddings to expand as they cook). Put the lids on top of the puddings, foil-side up, and secure with string.

5. Stand the moulds in a steamer and steam for 45 minutes. (Or use a large saucepan containing enough boiling water to come halfway up the sides of the moulds, topping up the boiling water as necessary during cooking.)

6. Remove the lids, then run the tip of a small, sharp knife around the edge of the puddings, to help release them. Invert them onto warmed plates and serve straight away, with custard.

HEREFORD APPLE DUMPLINGS

SERVES 4

Herefordshire is famous for its apple varieties and its farm ciders, both of which are used in cooking. In this rustic pudding, apples are cored, stuffed, then wrapped in pastry. The filling typically includes sultanas and marmalade but I've opted for a contemporary mix of dried cranberries, apricots and stem ginger. It's not really a traditional dumpling because it is baked rather than steamed, but it's delicious nonetheless. Serve hot, with custard or cream.

PASTRY

300g plain flour
A pinch of salt
150g unsalted butter, diced
About 4 tbsp ice-cold water
1 egg, lightly beaten, to glaze

FILLING

10g unsalted butter, softened
35g dried cranberries
35g dried apricots, finely diced
2 pieces of stem ginger in
  syrup, finely chopped, plus
  1 tbsp syrup from the jar
4 small cooking apples
4 tsp caster sugar, plus extra
  for sprinkling

STEP PHOTOGRAPHS
OVERLEAF

1. To make the pastry, put the flour and salt into a bowl, add the butter and rub in with your fingertips until the mix resembles fine breadcrumbs. Mix in enough water to bring the mix together, then gently knead it into a smooth ball. Wrap in cling film and leave to rest in the fridge for about 30 minutes.

2. Heat the oven to 200°C/Gas 6. Line a baking tray with baking parchment. For the filling, mix the butter, dried fruit, ginger and ginger syrup together in a bowl to combine. Set aside.

3. Peel and core the apples. Trim the bases to level, then use the peeler to shape each apple into a smooth sphere if necessary.

4. Divide the pastry into 4 pieces and roll out each one into a circle, 4–5mm thick. Check that the circles are big enough to cover the apples, then sprinkle each with 1 tsp caster sugar. Place an apple upside-down on each piece of pastry. Stuff the dried fruit mixture into the cavity of each apple.

5. Wrap the apples in the pastry by bringing the sides up around them and sealing the pastry edges together with a little water, trimming off the excess. Smooth the pastry over the apples with your hands. Turn the apples over so the join is underneath.

6. Roll out the pastry trimmings and cut out leaves. Use to decorate the apple parcels, sticking them on with a little water. Brush the pastry with beaten egg and sprinkle with sugar. Transfer the parcels to a baking tray and bake for 10 minutes, then lower the setting to 180°C/Gas 4 and bake for a further 30 minutes, until the pastry is golden brown. Serve hot, with cream or custard.

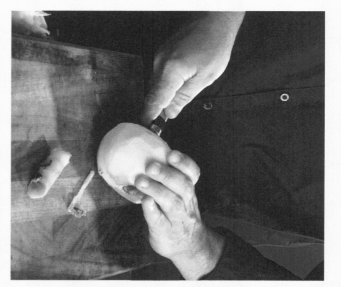

Pushing an apple corer through the stem end of the apple to the base, twisting it at the same time, to cut out the core.

Standing a smoothly trimmed apple on a sugar-sprinkled pastry round.

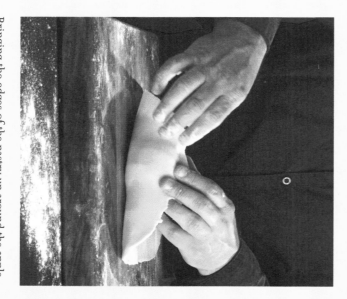

Bringing the edges of the pastry up around the apple to enclose it.

Pressing the dampened edges of the pastry together to seal the parcel.

Cutting out leaves from the pastry trimmings and marking veins with a small, sharp knife.

Sprinkling caster sugar over the egg-glazed parcel, ready for baking.

Smoothing the pastry neatly with the hands and turning it over so the seam is underneath.

Positioning the pastry leaf on the apple, using a little water to stick it in place.

BAKEWELL PUDDING

SERVES 6

Not to be confused with the tart of the same name (see page 130), Bakewell pudding consists of a puff pastry base spread with jam and filled with a rich, eggy mixture. Various inns in Bakewell claim to have invented it, but the Rutland Arms has the best claim. It isn't as elegant as a Bakewell tart and has even been unkindly compared to a cowpat, but I think it's lovely and it is very simple to make. The filling forms a dark crust in the oven, which soufflés up, then settles as the pudding cools.

1. Roll out the pastry and use to line a shallow 20cm cake tin (not a loose-bottomed one). Prick the base with a fork and chill in the fridge for 1 hour. Heat the oven to 180°C/Gas 4.

2. Spread the jam evenly over the pastry base. Beat the remaining ingredients together in a bowl until well combined and pour into the prepared case.

3. Bake for 45–50 minutes, until the filling is just set; keep a close eye on it to make sure the top doesn't brown too quickly and turn the oven down if it does.

4. Leave the pudding to cool completely before cutting into slices to serve.

200g good-quality ready-made all-butter puff pastry

FILLING

2 heaped tbsp raspberry jam
2 large eggs, plus 4 extra egg yolks
175g caster sugar
175g unsalted butter, melted
2 tbsp ground almonds

EQUIPMENT

A shallow 20cm cake tin (such as a sandwich tin)

If you like crumpets, you'll love these. A speciality of the Midlands, Wales and the North of England, pikelets have the characteristic holey top of a crumpet but are thinner and irregular in shape, as they are cooked free-form, like drop scones. They are very easy to make and taste delicious straight from the pan. They can also be served toasted the next day.

175g strong white bread flour
175g plain flour
2 x 7g sachets instant yeast
350ml milk
1 tsp caster sugar
½ tsp bicarbonate of soda
1 tsp salt
150–200ml warm water
A little sunflower oil, for cooking

EQUIPMENT

A flat griddle (or large heavy-based frying pan)

STEP PHOTOGRAPHS
OVERLEAF

1. Put the flours into a large bowl and stir in the yeast. Heat the milk to lukewarm and stir in the sugar until dissolved. Pour the milk mixture into the flour and mix well, then beat with a wooden spoon to make a smooth batter. This will take around 3–4 minutes and is hard work, but it is essential for creating the characteristic holes in the pikelets.

2. Cover the bowl with cling film and set aside in a warm place for about an hour. The batter will rise and then begin to fall; you'll see marks on the side of the bowl where it has dropped.

3. Mix the bicarbonate of soda and salt with 150ml warm water and beat into the rested batter. Gradually stir in enough of the remaining water to give a thick pouring consistency. Cover and leave to rest for 20 minutes. Small holes will appear on the surface and the mixture will become sticky.

4. Place a flat griddle or a large heavy-based frying pan over a medium heat. When it is hot, lightly grease it, using a wad of kitchen paper dipped in a little sunflower oil. You will need to cook the pikelets in batches. Drop 2 tbsp of the batter into the pan for each one. Cook for 2–3 minutes until the bubbles on the top have burst and the surface is set; the underside should be light brown. Turn them over and cook for 2 minutes more.

5. Serve immediately, with plenty of butter and jam or honey, or leave to cool and then toast.

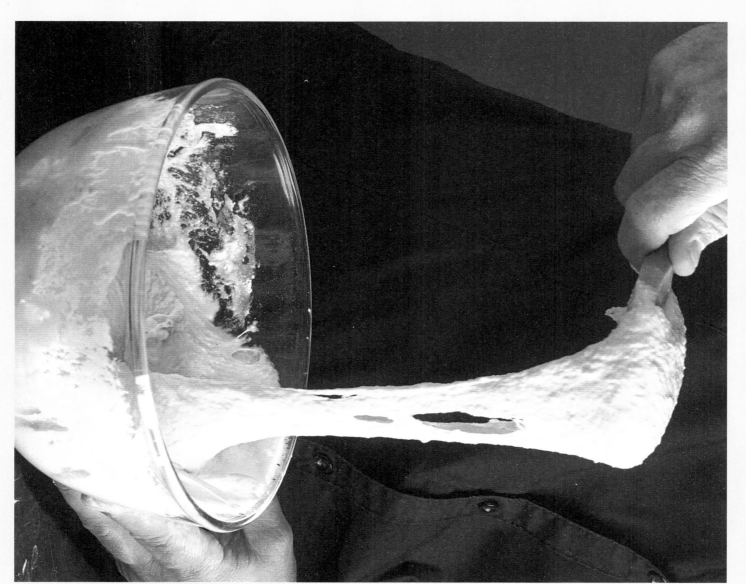

Beating the milk into the flour and yeast mixture with a wooden spoon to make a smooth batter and checking the consistency.

The yeast batter after its fermenting period; the marks around the side of the bowl show how it has risen and fallen during this time.

STAFFORDSHIRE OATCAKES

MAKES 8

These are more like pancakes than crisp Scottish-style oatcakes. Made from oatmeal and flour, the batter also contains yeast, which results in tiny bubbles on the surface. They were a staple food for workers in the Staffordshire potteries, who would buy them on their way to work. I trained as a potter and I like to imagine that they might have popped the oatcakes into the kilns to cook them. The intense heat would have ensured they retained their moisture and stayed soft. Eat them for breakfast or brunch, rolled around a savoury or sweet filling. My favourite is crisp bacon and cheese.

1. Heat the milk to lukewarm. Mix the flour, oatmeal and salt together in a bowl, then stir in the yeast. Gradually stir in the warm milk with a wooden spoon, then beat to form a batter. Cover and leave to stand for about 1½ hours, until the mixture begins to bubble and froth.

2. Add the melted butter to the mixture and use a stick blender to incorporate – this will get rid of any lumps of oatmeal. The batter should be a thick, pouring consistency; if it is too thick, add a splash of water.

3. Heat a heavy-based 20cm frying pan or pancake pan over a medium-high heat, then add a little butter or oil and swirl it around the pan.

4. Pour in about half a ladleful of batter, tilting the pan quickly so it covers the entire surface (if it is too thick to spread easily, add a little more water to the remaining batter). Cook for 1–2 minutes, until bubbles appear on the surface. Turn over and cook the other side for 1 minute or until lightly coloured. Remove to a warm plate and cook the rest in the same way.

5. Eat at once with your favourite topping, or stack the pancakes and keep them warm in a low oven.

400ml milk
100g plain flour
100g fine oatmeal
½ tsp salt
1 tsp instant yeast
15g unsalted butter, melted
A little butter or sunflower oil, for frying

EQUIPMENT

A 20cm frying pan or pancake pan

STILTON, PEAR AND WALNUT BREAD

MAKES 1 LARGE LOAF

One of the great regional cheeses of England, Stilton is made with local pasteurised milk in Derbyshire, Nottinghamshire and Leicestershire. Here it is used with pear and walnuts to flavour a gorgeous loaf of bread. Lovely alongside a bowl of celery soup, or as an addition to a winter buffet, it's also very good toasted.

500g strong white bread flour

10g salt

7g sachet instant yeast

20g unsalted butter, diced and softened

320ml water

200g Stilton cheese, crumbled

100g walnut pieces

1 pear, peeled, cored and diced

1. Tip the flour into a large bowl. Add the salt to one side, the yeast to the other. Add the butter and three-quarters of the water, then turn the mixture with the fingers of one hand. Add the remaining water a little at a time, continuing to mix until all the flour is taken in and the dough is soft and slightly sticky; you might not need all the water.

2. Coat the work surface with a little oil to prevent the dough sticking. Turn out the dough and knead for at least 5 minutes, until it is smooth and no longer sticky. Lightly oil the bowl, return the dough to it and cover with cling film. Leave to rise for at least an hour, until doubled in size.

3. Line a baking tray with baking parchment. Scrape the dough out of the bowl onto a lightly floured surface and fold it inwards repeatedly until all the air is knocked out and it is smooth. Add the Stilton, walnut and pear pieces to the dough and work them in well.

4. Shape the dough into a rectangle about 30cm long, roll it up into a sausage, then flatten it out again and roll it up a bit tighter this time. Tuck the edges underneath and neaten the loaf by rolling the edges to taper them slightly. Put the dough on the prepared tray with the join underneath. Place the tray in a plastic bag and leave to prove for about 40 minutes, until the loaf has doubled in size. Heat the oven to 200°C/Gas 6.

5. Just before baking, gently rub flour all over the loaf, then make deep diagonal cuts along the top, first in one direction, then the other, to form a criss-cross pattern. Bake for 30 minutes, until well risen and golden brown. Cool on a wire rack.

LINCOLNSHIRE PLUM BREAD

MAKES 1 SMALL LOAF

250g strong white bread flour
¼ tsp ground mixed spice
¼ tsp salt
25g dark soft brown sugar
7g sachet instant yeast
15g lard
10g unsalted butter
1 medium egg
100ml water
100g mixed dried fruit
50g pitted prunes, chopped

EQUIPMENT
A 500g loaf tin

'Plum' can refer to dried fruit, and this lightly spiced loaf is often made with just currants and sultanas. I've added some prunes here, so the plum is present after all. An authentic Lincolnshire plum bread is always made with lard, a legacy of the time when most cottagers kept a pig. Thanks to the lard, which helps to keep the crumb structure soft, this loaf should keep for at least a week.

1. Mix the flour and spice in a bowl. Add the salt and sugar to one side, the yeast to the other. Rub in the lard and butter with your fingertips. Mix the egg with 50ml water, add to the mixture and turn with the fingers of one hand. Add the remaining water a little at a time, mixing until all the flour is taken in and you have a soft, slightly sticky dough; you might not need all the water.

2. Oil the work surface to prevent sticking and knead the dough on it for at least 5 minutes, until smooth and no longer sticky. Lightly oil the bowl, return the dough to it and cover with cling film. Leave to rise until at least doubled in size, 1½–2 hours.

3. Tip the risen dough out onto a lightly oiled surface. Add all the dried fruit and knead it gently into the dough. Return the dough to the bowl, cover and leave to prove for 1 hour.

4. Grease a 500g loaf tin with a little lard. Scrape the risen dough out onto a lightly floured surface and fold it inwards repeatedly until all the air is knocked out and the dough is smooth.

5. Shape into an oblong by flattening out slightly and folding the sides into the middle. Roll the whole lot up – the top should be smooth, with the seam underneath. Place the dough in the prepared tin. Put the tin into a plastic bag and leave to prove for about an hour, until risen. Heat the oven to 200°C/Gas 6.

6. Bake the loaf for 25 minutes, then lower the oven setting to 180°C/Gas 4 and bake for a further 10–15 minutes, until the crust is golden brown and the base of the loaf sounds hollow when tapped. Remove from the tin and leave to cool on a wire rack. Serve sliced and buttered.

Forget supermarket versions — home-made is the way to go with this popular tart. I've included fresh raspberries here for a sharp contrast to the sweetness of the frangipane. A teatime treat, it's also lovely as a dessert with cream. I usually make it in an oblong tin to slice into fingers, but it works well in a 23cm round tin too.

PASTRY

200g plain flour

2 tbsp icing sugar

100g cold unsalted butter, diced

1 medium egg

1 tsp lemon juice

2–3 tsp ice-cold water

FRANGIPANE FILLING

100g unsalted butter

100g caster sugar

2 large eggs

50g plain flour

75g ground almonds

A drop of almond extract
(optional)

100g raspberry jam

100g raspberries

20g flaked almonds

TO FINISH

Icing sugar, for dusting

EQUIPMENT

A 36 x 12cm rectangular tart tin
(or 23cm round tart tin)

STEP PHOTOGRAPHS
OVERLEAF

1. To make the pastry, mix the flour and icing sugar together in a bowl. Add the butter and rub it in lightly with your fingertips until the mixture resembles fine breadcrumbs. Mix the egg with the lemon juice and 2 tsp water. Stir into the mixture with a round-bladed knife, adding another 1 tsp water if necessary. (Alternatively you can make it in a food processor, blitzing the flour, icing sugar and butter together, then adding the liquid.)

2. As the dough comes together, gently knead it into a smooth ball. Wrap in cling film and chill for at least 15 minutes.

3. Heat the oven to 200°C/Gas 6. Roll out the pastry on a lightly floured surface to a 3mm thickness and use to line a 36 x 12cm loose-bottomed tart tin (or a 23cm round tin), leaving a little excess overhanging the edge.

4. Line the pastry case with baking parchment and fill with baking beans or dried beans. Bake blind for 12–15 minutes, until the pastry is dry to the touch. Remove the paper and beans and return the pastry case to the oven for about 5 minutes until very lightly coloured. Trim away excess pastry from the edge. Turn the oven down to 180°C/Gas 4.

5. For the frangipane filling, beat the butter and sugar together until light and fluffy, then beat in the eggs one at a time. Stir in the flour, ground almonds and the almond extract, if using.

6. Spread the jam over the base of the pastry case and scatter over the raspberries. Top with the frangipane and spread evenly. Bake for 10 minutes, then scatter the flaked almonds on top and cook for a further 15 minutes until the filling is golden. Leave to cool in the tin before slicing. Dust with icing sugar to serve.

Rolling out the pastry on a lightly floured surface to a rectangle, about 3mm thick, large enough to line the tart tin.

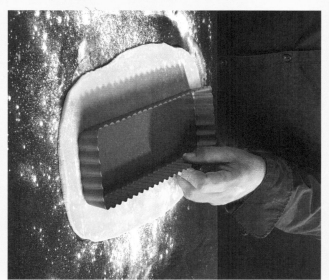

Checking the pastry rectangle is large enough to line the base and sides of the tart tin.

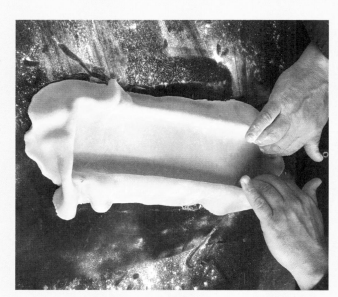

Lining the tart tin with the pastry and pressing it neatly into the edges and corners.

Filling the parchment-lined pastry case with a layer of baking beans, ready to bake blind (i.e. without its filling) to stop the base rising up.

Spreading the raspberry jam evenly over the base of the pastry case with the back of a spoon.

Gently spreading the frangipane with a small palette knife to level the surface.

Trimming away excess pastry from the edge of the baked pastry case, using a small, sharp knife.

Spooning the frangipane filling on top of the fresh raspberries in the pastry case.

NORTHAMPTONSHIRE CHEESECAKES

MAKES 10

If you are from Yorkshire, you'll immediately recognise that these are very similar to curd tarts. There are many recipes for baked cheesecakes in the Midlands. Best eaten fresh, they are beautifully light and bear little resemblance to what we usually think of as cheesecake these days. I like them with a hint of lemon but you could add a splash of almond extract instead. If you can't get curd cheese, ricotta makes a good substitute.

1. To make the pastry, put the flour and icing sugar into a bowl and mix well. Add the butter and rub it in lightly with your fingertips until the mixture resembles fine breadcrumbs. Mix the egg yolk with the lemon juice and 2 tsp ice-cold water. Add to the mixture and stir in with a round-bladed knife, adding another 1 tsp water if necessary. (Alternatively you can make the pastry in a food processor, blitzing the flour, icing sugar and butter together, then adding the liquid.)

2. When the dough begins to stick together, gently knead it into a smooth ball. Wrap the pastry in cling film and chill for at least 15 minutes.

3. Heat the oven to 180°C/Gas 4. Roll out the pastry on a lightly floured surface to a 2–3mm thickness. Cut out 10 circles using a 10cm cutter, re-rolling the trimmings to cut more as necessary. Use the pastry rounds to line 10 holes of a muffin tray.

4. Divide the currants between the pastry cases. Put the sugar, curd cheese, eggs, egg yolks, lemon zest and melted butter in a bowl and beat with a wooden spoon until smooth. Transfer to a jug.

5. Pour the mixture into the pastry cases and grate a little nutmeg over the surface. Bake for 20–25 minutes, until the filling is just set and the pastry is golden. The cheesecakes are easiest to turn out of the tins when they are still slightly warm.

SWEET PASTRY

150g plain flour
2 tbsp icing sugar
75g cold unsalted butter, diced
1 egg yolk
½ tsp lemon juice
2–3 tsp ice-cold water

FILLING

85g currants
50g caster sugar
225g curd cheese
2 medium eggs, plus 2 extra egg yolks
Grated zest of 1 lemon
25g unsalted butter, melted
A little grated nutmeg

EQUIPMENT

A 10- or 12-hole muffin tray
A 10cm pastry cutter

MELTON HUNT CAKE

MAKES A 15CM CAKE

Melton Mowbray in Leicestershire is most famous for its pork pies, but this deep, rich fruit cake, with its topping of glacé cherries and split almonds, also deserves attention. First made in 1854, it was traditionally eaten by the Melton Hunt, washed down with port or sherry from a stirrup cup. Like all rich fruit cakes, it improves as it matures.

175g unsalted butter, well
    softened
175g dark muscovado sugar
Grated zest of 1 lemon
3 medium eggs
175g plain flour
175g sultanas
75g currants
75g glacé cherries, halved,
    plus extra to decorate
75g flaked almonds
2 tbsp dark rum
8–10 blanched split almonds,
    to decorate

EQUIPMENT

A deep 15cm round cake tin

1. Heat the oven to 150°C/Gas 2. Grease a deep 15cm round cake tin and line the base and sides with baking parchment, extending the parchment high above the rim to protect the cake during cooking.

2. Using a handheld electric whisk, beat the butter, sugar and lemon zest together until fluffy, then beat in the eggs one at a time, adding a spoonful of the flour with the last egg if it threatens to curdle.

3. Sift in the remaining flour and fold it in using a large metal spoon. Fold in the sultanas, currants, glacé cherries and flaked almonds, followed by the rum.

4. Spoon the mixture into the prepared tin and level the surface. Decorate the top with concentric circles of split almonds and halved glacé cherries, gently pushing them into the cake mixture a little.

5. Bake on the middle shelf of the oven for 45 minutes, then lower the oven setting to 140°C/Gas 1. Bake for a further 1½–1¾ hours, until a skewer inserted in the centre comes out clean; if the top browns too much before the cake is done, cover it loosely with a sheet of baking parchment or foil.

6. Leave the cake to cool completely in the tin before turning out.

JUMBLES

MAKES 10

100g plain flour
60g caster sugar
25g unsalted butter, diced
25g ground almonds
Grated zest of 1 lemon
30–40ml milk

LEMON ICING

50g icing sugar
1 tbsp lemon juice

EQUIPMENT

A greaseproof paper piping bag

STEP PHOTOGRAPHS
OVERLEAF

Sometimes known as Bosworth jumbles, these were reputedly a favourite of Richard III, and legend has it that the recipe was found on Bosworth battlefield after he died. I'm not entirely convinced that soldiers went into battle armed with biscuit recipes but there's no denying that these are very good biscuits indeed. Traditionally they are twisted into knots, figures-of-eight or S shapes before baking. I have added a little lemon icing for a zesty note.

1. Put the flour into a bowl and stir in the sugar. Add the butter and rub it in with your fingertips until the mixture resembles fine breadcrumbs. Stir in the ground almonds and lemon zest, followed by enough milk to bring the mixture together into a soft dough. Wrap in cling film and chill for 30 minutes.

2. Heat the oven to 180°C/Gas 4. Line a baking tray with baking parchment.

3. Roll the dough into a cylinder and cut into 10 even pieces. On a lightly floured surface, with your hands, roll each one into a rope, 7mm in diameter. Twist and knot them into any shapes you like. If you prefer, you can make the pieces thicker and bend them into S shapes.

4. Using a palette knife, carefully lift the dough shapes onto the lined baking tray, spacing them slightly apart. Bake for 12–15 minutes, until pale golden. Leave on the baking tray for a few minutes to cool slightly and firm up, then transfer to a wire rack and leave to cool completely.

5. For the icing, mix the icing sugar and lemon juice together in a bowl to make a smooth icing. Put into a greaseproof paper piping bag, snip off the end and pipe it randomly over the jumbles – or just drizzle it over with a teaspoon if you prefer.

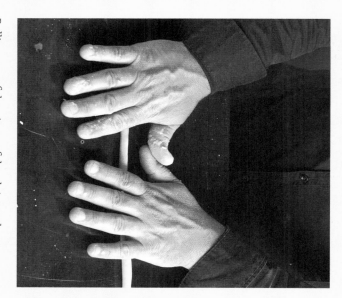

Rolling one of the pieces of dough into a long rope, about 7mm in diameter.

Folding and shaping the rope of dough into a figure-of-eight.

Adding enough milk to the mixture to bring it together and form a soft dough.

Dividing the rested dough into 10 even-sized pieces, ready for shaping.

Bending slightly thicker ropes of jumble dough into S shapes.

Originally 'Shrewsbury cakes,' these delectable little biscuits have been around since the 1700s, when they were often flavoured with cinnamon, nutmeg and rosewater. My recipe includes currants, a 19th century addition. As the dough is delicate and buttery, it can be a little tricky to work with, so chill it thoroughly.

100g unsalted butter, softened
100g caster sugar, plus extra for dusting
Grated zest of 1 lemon
1 medium egg
200g plain flour
50g currants

EQUIPMENT
A 6.5cm fluted pastry cutter

1. Put the butter, sugar and lemon zest into a bowl and beat until pale and fluffy. Beat in the egg, then stir in the flour and currants until thoroughly combined. Turn out onto a lightly floured surface and knead briefly until smooth. Wrap in cling film and chill in the fridge for about an hour.

2. Heat the oven to 180°C/Gas 4. Line 2 baking trays with baking parchment.

3. On a floured surface, roll the dough out to a 5mm thickness — it's quite soft, so work quickly and flour the work surface well if necessary. Using a 6.5cm fluted cutter, stamp out biscuits and place them on the baking trays, then sprinkle with extra caster sugar. Press the trimmings together and re-roll them to make more biscuits.

4. Bake for 10–12 minutes, until the biscuits are firm and a very pale brown colour. Leave on the baking trays for a few minutes to cool slightly and firm up a little more, then transfer to a wire rack and leave to cool completely.

THE —
NORTH

Alnwick
CARLISLE
NEWCASTLE
Keswick
CUMBRIA
MIDDLESBOROUGH
LAKE DISTRICT
Kendal
Whitby
NORTH YORK MOORS
WENSLEYDALE
YORKSHIRE DALES
Ripon
YORKSHIRE
HARROGATE
Goosnargh
BLACKPOOL
LANCASHIRE
YORK
LEEDS
Chorley
Morley
Rothwell
HULL
Eccles
MANCHESTER
Wakefield
LIVERPOOL
Denby Dale
CHESTER

Pies and pastries, gingerbreads and fruit cakes, outsized rolls such as stottie cakes – this is big food for big appetites. It's hardly accidental that the North of England is the area that invented the high tea. No messing about with finger sandwiches and miniature cakes, high tea is a feast that will restore you after a long, hard day. It is thought to have developed in response to the needs of factory workers, who would arrive home famished at around 6pm, but the traditional farmhouse high tea is an important feature of rural life too.

Although high tea usually features cold meats, eggs, cheese and salads, it's the baked goods that take pride of place, with the table positively groaning under the weight of bacon and egg tarts, sturdy plate pies, scones, fruit cake, filled rolls and piles of bread and butter – all washed down by a large, endlessly refillable pot of tea.

There is no denying that northerners love their food. Life in the North, whether for farm or factory workers, has always been tough, the climate bracing to say the least, and the hills, dales and moorland inhospitable in winter. Food really is fuel here, and northern thriftiness means that nothing goes to waste. Northern women have always had a reputation for being great bakers. They have a deft, light touch when it comes to pastry, and enough elbow grease to beat up cake batters by hand without any trouble at all. In the past, it was the custom to set one day a week aside for baking – I bet that day was eagerly awaited by the whole family.

It's impossible to imagine the food of the North without pies: the Eccles and Chorley cakes of Lancashire (pages 168 and 173), the meat and potato pies that are found throughout the region (such as the Denby Dale pie on page 153) and the lovely fruit plate pies of Yorkshire (see the rhubarb pie on page 158). Made with whatever was in season – rhubarb, gooseberries, apples, or bilberries gathered from the moors – plate pies are a classic example of frugality producing something utterly delicious. And don't forget the Yorkshire habit of eating pies or fruit cake with a piece of crumbly Wensleydale cheese:'An apple pie without cheese is like a kiss without a squeeze.'

A traditional working port, Whitby has some outstanding fish and chip shops overlooking the harbour, so you can watch the fish being unloaded while you eat. This is a pretty luxurious pie. In the past it would have been made with whatever was landed on the day. Making the pastry lattice top is fun but, if it's all too much, you could just cover the pie with a pastry lid in the usual way.

PASTRY

275g plain flour

A pinch of salt

135g cold unsalted butter, diced

1 medium egg, plus 1 egg, lightly beaten, to glaze

1 tbsp ice-cold water

FILLING

700ml full-fat milk

1 bay leaf

1 small onion, peeled and halved

4 cloves

60g unsalted butter

60g plain flour

75g spinach, roughly chopped

2 tbsp chopped parsley

400g haddock fillet, skinned

400g smoked haddock fillet, skinned

175g cooked peeled prawns

Salt and pepper

EQUIPMENT

A 1.2 litre pie dish

STEP PHOTOGRAPHS
OVERLEAF

1. To make the pastry, put the flour and salt into a bowl and rub in the butter with your fingertips until the mix resembles fine breadcrumbs. Mix the egg with the water and stir into the mixture with a round-bladed knife until it forms a dough, adding a little more water if necessary. Knead briefly until smooth, wrap in cling film and chill for at least 30 minutes.

2. Put the milk in a pan with the bay leaf and onion studded with the cloves. Bring slowly to the boil, turn off the heat and leave to infuse for at least 30 minutes. Strain the milk into a jug.

3. Melt the butter in a pan, stir in the flour and cook gently for a few minutes, then gradually stir in the infused milk. Increase the heat a little, bring to a simmer and cook, stirring, for a few minutes. Add the spinach, parsley and some salt and pepper.

4. Check the fish for pin bones, then cut into bite-sized pieces and put into a 1.2 litre pie dish with the prawns. Pour on the sauce, gently mix with the fish and check the seasoning. Leave to cool.

5. Heat the oven to 200°C/Gas 6. Roll out the pastry on a lightly floured surface to a 3mm thickness, and a little larger than the top of the pie dish. Use to form the lattice (as shown overleaf).

6. Dampen the rim of the pie dish with water, cut a strip of pastry to fit round it and gently press it on. Brush with a little water, then invert the lattice from the parchment onto the dish. Press the ends of the strips onto the pastry rim and trim the edges.

7. Brush the top of the lattice with beaten egg to glaze and bake the pie for 25–30 minutes, until the pastry is golden brown.

Cutting the pastry into 1cm wide strips for the lattice pie topping (you will need 12–14 strips in total).

Weaving the pastry strips on a sheet of baking parchment to form a lattice (this makes it easier to lift the lattice on top of the pie).

Gently pressing a dampened strip of pastry onto the rim of the pie dish.

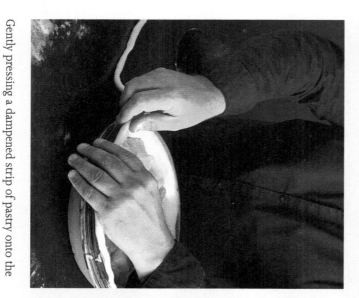

Carefully inverting the pastry lattice onto the top of the pie.

Trimming away the excess ends of the pastry lattice, using a small, sharp knife.

DENBY DALE PIE

SERVES 4–6

Meat and potato pies are distinctly northern in character and this particular filling is my long-term favourite. Denby Dale in West Yorkshire is famous for baking giant pies – not least a 12-tonne pie, 12 metres long, which was made to celebrate the millennium.

FILLING

2 large onions, chopped
700g chuck (braising steak), cut into 4–5cm chunks
400g waxy potatoes, such as Estima or Maris Peer, peeled and cut into 4cm chunks
400g floury potatoes, such as King Edward, peeled and cut into 4cm chunks
A few drops of gravy browning
Salt and pepper

PASTRY

275g plain flour
A pinch of salt
135g cold unsalted butter, diced
1 medium egg, plus 1 egg, lightly beaten, to glaze
1 tbsp ice-cold water

EQUIPMENT

A 1.2–1.4 litre pie dish

1. To make the filling, put the onions and meat in a large pan, add enough water just to cover and bring to a simmer. Cover, lower the heat and simmer very gently for 1½ hours. Add both types of potato with some salt and pepper and cook for a further 30–35 minutes, until they are soft and the meat tender. The floury potatoes should have collapsed and thickened the juices. Stir in the gravy browning and take off the heat.

2. Adjust the seasoning, then pour off 300–600ml of the gravy into a jug (enough to leave the filling moist but not swimming in liquid). Keep this to serve with the pie. Transfer the filling to 1.2–1.4 litre pie dish and leave to cool completely.

3. To make the pastry, put the flour and salt into a bowl and rub in the butter with your fingertips until the mix resembles fine breadcrumbs. Mix the egg with the water, add to the mixture and stir with a round-bladed knife until it forms a dough, adding a little more water if needed. Knead briefly until smooth, wrap in cling film and chill for at least 30 minutes. Heat the oven to 200°C/Gas 6.

4. On a lightly floured surface, roll out the pastry to a 5–6mm thickness. Cut a 2cm wide strip. Dampen the rim of the pie dish, stick the pastry strip onto it and brush it with a little water.

5. Lay the pastry on top of the pie and trim off the excess. Press down to seal the edges. Use the pastry trimmings to make decorations, if you like. Brush the pastry lid with beaten egg, add any decorations and brush these too. Make a couple of small holes in the centre to let out steam during baking.

6. Bake the pie for 30–40 minutes, until the pastry is golden brown. Leave to stand for 10–15 minutes before serving.

I'm very fond of the French 'crown', because it's a great way of getting flavour into a dough. It's also an excellent use for the air-dried ham now produced – along with salamis and chorizo – by artisan producers in Cumbria and elsewhere in the country. And if you can get a local goat's cheese too, so much the better.

250g strong white bread flour

1 tsp salt

7g sachet instant yeast

50g unsalted butter, diced and softened

1 medium egg, lightly beaten

135ml warm full-fat milk

FILLING

8–10 slices of Cumbrian air-dried ham

250g soft goat's cheese

15 basil leaves, shredded

STEP PHOTOGRAPHS
OVERLEAF

1. Put the flour into a large bowl and add the salt on one side, the yeast on the other. Add the butter, egg and two-thirds of the milk, then turn the mixture with the fingers of one hand. Add the remaining milk a little at a time, continuing to mix until all the flour from the side is taken in and the dough is soft and slightly sticky; you might not need all the milk.

2. Transfer the dough to a lightly floured surface and knead it for 5–10 minutes. Initially the dough will be sticky but it will become easier to work as you continue to knead. When it feels smooth and silky, put it into a lightly oiled bowl, cover and leave to rise for about an hour, until doubled in size.

3. Line a baking tray with baking parchment. Turn the risen dough out onto a lightly floured surface. Without knocking back, roll it into a rectangle about 33 x 25cm. Turn the dough, if necessary, so you have a long edge facing you. Lay the ham slices over the dough. Break the goat's cheese into pieces and scatter them over the ham, then sprinkle over the basil.

4. Starting at a long edge, roll the dough up tightly, like a Swiss roll. Roll it back and forth a little to seal, then cut it in half lengthways, leaving it joined at the top. Twist the 2 dough lengths together, as if wringing out a cloth, then join the ends to form a circle. Transfer to the lined baking tray.

5. Place the baking tray inside a clean plastic bag and leave the couronne to prove until doubled in size. Heat the oven to 200°C/Gas 6.

6. Bake the couronne for 25 minutes until risen and golden brown. Leave to cool on a wire rack.

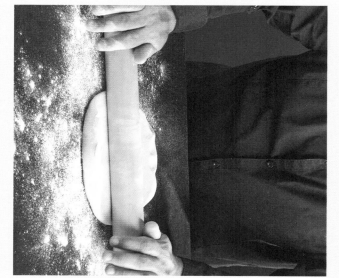

Rolling out the risen dough (without first 'knocking back') on a lightly floured surface.

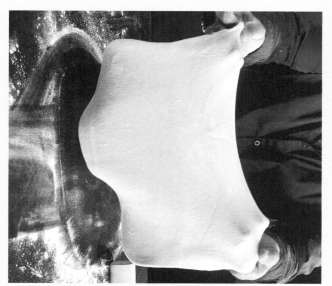

Continuing to roll out the dough to a large rectangle, 33 x 25cm, lifting the pliable dough from time to time to check it isn't sticking.

Scattering the goat's cheese over the air-dried ham slices on the dough.

Rolling up the dough tightly, from a long edge, to enclose the filling.

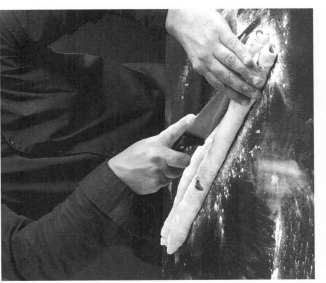

Cutting the roll in half lengthways with a large, sharp knife, leaving it attached at one end.

Bringing the two ends of the dough together and pressing them together to seal and form a circle.

Rolling the dough parcel back and forth to seal the edges.

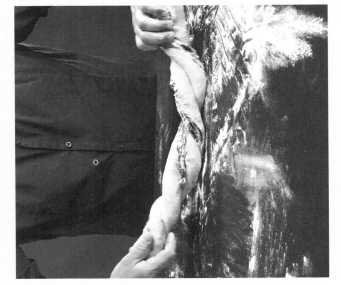

Twisting the two pieces of dough together really tightly to get a well-shaped loaf.

Yorkshire forced rhubarb, grown in the Rhubarb Triangle between Wakefield, Morley and Rothwell since the 1870s, is highly prized. It is cultivated in the dark in forcing sheds, whose warmth tricks the plants into behaving as if spring has come. The resulting tender stalks of rhubarb are harvested by candlelight – an amazing sight.

A plate pie is a very British thing. Enamel plates are perfect to use, as they conduct the heat so well, which helps you to avoid that soggy-bottom issue. Forced rhubarb is sweeter than outdoor-grown, so you can reduce the sugar in the filling if using it here.

PASTRY

275g plain flour
2 tbsp icing sugar
140g cold unsalted butter, diced
3–4 tbsp ice-cold water
1 egg, lightly beaten, to glaze

FILLING

450g rhubarb, cut into 1cm chunks
2 tbsp custard powder
1 tsp ground ginger
130g caster sugar, plus extra for sprinkling
1 tbsp semolina

EQUIPMENT

A 24cm pie plate

1. For the pastry, put the flour and icing sugar into a bowl, add the butter and rub it in with your fingertips until the mixture resembles fine breadcrumbs. Stir in just enough water to bring it together into a dough. Knead briefly until smooth, wrap in cling film and leave to rest in the fridge for 30 minutes.

2. Heat the oven to 200°C/Gas 6. Set aside about a third of the pastry. Roll out the remainder on a lightly floured surface to a 2–3mm thickness and use to line a 24cm pie plate. Roll out the remaining pastry to form a lid.

3. For the filling, mix the rhubarb with the custard powder, ginger and caster sugar. Sprinkle the semolina over the pastry base, then spoon the rhubarb mixture evenly on top.

4. Brush the edges of the pastry with a little beaten egg, then position the pastry lid on top of the pie. Trim off the excess pastry, press the edges together to seal, then crimp. Use the pastry trimmings to make decorations, if you like.

5. Brush the top of the pie with beaten egg, add any decorations and brush these too. Make 3 small slits in the top to let the steam out. Sprinkle evenly with caster sugar.

6. Bake for 15 minutes, then lower the oven setting to 180°C/Gas 4 and cook for a further 25 minutes, until the rhubarb is tender and the pastry is golden brown. Leave to rest for 15 minutes before serving with custard, cream or ice cream.

MANCHESTER TART

SERVES 6

I grew up eating this tart at school and swore I'd never eat it again, but I've come back to it now. Made well, it's lovely. This is a deluxe version, with light, crisp pastry and a proper pastry cream filling made with egg yolks and, for a slight twist, coconut milk.

1. For the pastry, put the flour and icing sugar into a bowl and rub in the butter with your fingertips until the mixture resembles fine breadcrumbs. Mix the egg with the lemon juice and 2 tsp water and stir into the flour mix with a round-bladed knife, adding a little more water if necessary. As it begins to form a dough, gently knead into a smooth ball. Wrap in cling film and chill for at least 15 minutes.

2. Heat the oven to 200°C/Gas 6. Roll out the pastry on a lightly floured surface to a 3mm thickness and use it to line a 23cm loose-bottomed tart tin, leaving a little excess overhanging the edge. Keep a small piece of uncooked pastry back in case you need to patch any cracks later.

3. Line the pastry case with baking parchment, fill with baking beans and bake blind for 12–15 minutes, until the pastry is dry. Remove the paper and beans and return the pastry case to the oven for 5 minutes or until very lightly coloured. Trim excess pastry from the edge. Patch any cracks with a little raw pastry.

4. Pour the coconut milk into a pan. Scrape the vanilla seeds from the pod and add them to the pan. Slowly bring just to the boil. Meanwhile, beat the egg yolks, sugar and flour together in a bowl. Slowly pour on the hot coconut milk, stirring. Pour back into the pan and bring slowly to a simmer, stirring over a low heat. Cook, stirring, for 5 minutes, until it is very thick and the raw flour taste has been cooked out. Remove from the heat.

5. Spread the jam over the cooled pastry base and arrange the banana slices on top. Pour over the custard. Toast the coconut briefly in a dry frying pan until golden, then sprinkle over the custard. Refrigerate to set for at least an hour before serving.

PASTRY

200g plain flour
2 tbsp icing sugar
100g cold unsalted butter, diced
1 medium egg
1 tsp lemon juice
2–3 tsp ice-cold water

FILLING

400g tin coconut milk
1 vanilla pod, slit lengthways
6 egg yolks
125g caster sugar
3 tbsp plain flour
150g raspberry jam
2–3 bananas, peeled and sliced
50g desiccated coconut

EQUIPMENT

A 23cm loose-bottomed round tart tin

My Dad used to make these in the bakery – they're known as barm cakes in other parts of the country. On Tyneside, though, they are called stotties – meaning 'to bounce' in Geordie. These sturdy bread rolls, the size of a dinner plate, are traditionally baked on the floor of the oven after just one rising, making them firmer and denser than other white breads. They were supposedly 'stotted' or bounced on the bakery floor to check that they were done. I have to admit that my recipe includes a brief second rising for a lighter result. Fill them as you would a classic stottie – with roast meat, pease pudding and ham, bacon and eggs, or other hearty fillings.

500g strong white bread flour
7g salt
40g caster sugar
7g sachet instant yeast
40g lard, diced
320ml water

1. Put the flour in a large bowl and add the salt and sugar on one side, the yeast on the other. Add the lard and three-quarters of the water, then turn the mixture round with the fingers of one hand. Add the remaining water a little at a time, continuing to mix until all the flour from the side of the bowl is taken in and you have a soft dough; you might not need all the water.

2. Coat the work surface with a little oil to prevent the dough sticking. Turn out the dough onto the surface and knead for at least 5 minutes, until it is smooth and silky. Lightly oil the bowl, return the dough to it and cover with cling film. Leave to rise for at least an hour, until doubled in size. Line 2 baking trays with baking parchment.

3. Scrape the dough out of the bowl onto a lightly floured surface and fold it inwards repeatedly until it is smooth and all the air has been knocked out.

4. Divide in half and press each piece out into a circle, roughly 20cm in diameter. Place on the prepared baking trays, cover and leave to rise for 30 minutes. Heat the oven to 220°C/Gas 7.

5. Just before baking, make indentations all over the surface of each stottie with your finger and dust lightly with flour. Bake for 15–20 minutes until golden brown. Transfer to a wire rack to cool.

WHITBY LEMON BUNS

MAKES 10

These are sold by several Yorkshire bakeries – including Botham's of Whitby, which is credited with their invention. Although they usually contain sultanas, I've gone for candied lemon peel to echo the lemon glacé icing. Locals split them in half before eating and then turn the top over so the icing is inside, like a sandwich.

400g strong white bread flour

5g salt

40g caster sugar

2 x 7g sachets instant yeast

40g unsalted butter, diced and softened

120ml milk

120ml water

Grated zest of 1 lemon

100g candied lemon peel, finely diced

LEMON ICING

200g icing sugar

Juice of 1 lemon (approx)

STEP PHOTOGRAPHS OVERLEAF

1. Put the flour in a large bowl and add the salt and sugar on one side, the yeast on the other. Add the butter and milk, then turn the mixture round with the fingers of one hand. Add the water a little at a time, continuing to mix until you have taken in all the flour from the side of the bowl and the dough is soft and slightly sticky; you might not need all the water.

2. Coat the work surface with a little oil to prevent the dough sticking. Turn out the dough and knead for at least 5 minutes, until it is smooth and no longer sticky. Lightly oil the bowl, return the dough to it and cover with cling film. Leave to rise for at least an hour, until doubled in size.

3. Add the lemon zest and candied peel to the dough and work in to incorporate evenly. Transfer the dough to a lightly floured surface and fold it inwards repeatedly until all the air is knocked out and the dough is smooth. Form into a long roll.

4. Line a baking tray with baking parchment. Divide the dough into 10 pieces and roll each one into a ball (as shown overleaf). Place on the prepared baking tray, arranging them close together. As they rise, the buns will touch each other. Place the tray in a clean plastic bag and leave to prove for about 40 minutes, until the buns have doubled in size. Heat the oven to 220°C/Gas 7.

5. Bake the buns for 15–20 minutes, until they are golden and sound hollow when tapped underneath. Cool on a wire rack.

6. For the icing, mix the icing sugar with enough lemon juice to give a fairly thick, pourable consistency. Separate the buns and dip the top of each bun into the icing, then place on a wire rack and leave to set. The buns are best eaten within 24 hours.

Transferring the dough, with the lemon zest and candied peel evenly distributed, to a lightly floured surface ready for 'knocking back'.

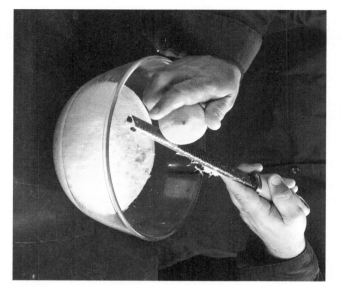

Grating the lemon zest onto the risen dough, using a fine Microplane grater.

Folding the dough inwards repeatedly and pressing it to flatten, to knock out all the air.

Working the lemon zest and candied peel into the dough with one hand.

Cutting the dough into 10 even-sized pieces.

Forming the dough into a long roll.

Arranging the balls of dough close together on the parchment-lined baking tray, ready for proving.

Forming a cage over a piece of dough and moving the hand in a circular motion, to rotate the dough rapidly and shape it into a neat ball.

Making these gorgeous currant-filled pastries was one of my first jobs at the bakery and I had one every day for breakfast for four years. Lancastrians refer to Eccles cakes, with typical Northern humour, as dead-fly pies, and to a large pastry filled with currants and cut into squares as flies' graveyard, but Eccles cakes are up there amongst the greats – especially if you take the trouble to make your own.

500g good-quality ready-made all-butter puff pastry
A little milk, for brushing

FILLING

150g currants
20g unsalted butter, melted
50g caster sugar, plus extra for sprinkling
Grated zest of 1 lemon
Freshly grated nutmeg

EQUIPMENT

A 10cm pastry cutter

STEP PHOTOGRAPHS
OVERLEAF

1. For the filling, wash the currants and dry them really well. Place in a bowl, add the melted butter and turn to coat them. Stir in the sugar, lemon zest and nutmeg.

2. Roll out the puff pastry on a lightly floured surface to a 5mm thickness. Stamp out rounds with a 10cm cutter, then place a heaped tablespoonful of the currant mixture in the centre of each one. Brush the rim of each circle with a little water. Gather the pastry edges up over the filling and press together to seal.

3. Turn each Eccles cake over so the seam is now underneath. Press gently with your hand to flatten slightly. Place on a baking tray and leave to rest in the fridge for 30 minutes. Heat the oven to 200°C/Gas 6.

4. Brush the Eccles cakes with a little milk, then make 3 slashes in the top of each one with a sharp knife to expose the fruit. Sprinkle with caster sugar and bake for 15–20 minutes, until the pastry is golden brown. Leave to cool on a wire rack until still just warm, or completely.

Stamping out rounds from the rolled-out pastry, using a 10cm cutter.

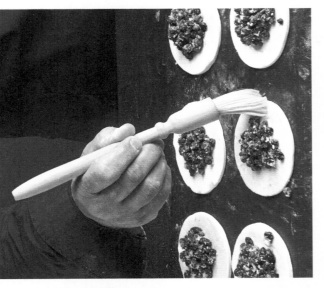

Brushing the pastry around the filling with a little water.

Turning the pastries over, so the seam is underneath, and pressing them gently to flatten slightly.

Releasing the pastry rounds from the cutter.

Gathering the pastry edges up over the filling and pressing them together to seal.

CHORLEY CAKES

MAKES 10

These are similar to the more familiar Eccles cakes on page 168, but they are made with shortcrust rather than flaky pastry and tend to be less sweet. You need to keep the pastry nice and short, so don't overwork it. I've taken the liberty of soaking the currants in orange liqueur and adding a little orange zest for a citrus twist.

Lovely served warm from the oven as a pudding with cream or ice cream, these pastries also keep well in a tin to have for tea.

1. For the filling, mix the currants with the orange liqueur and leave to soak overnight. The next day add the sugar and orange zest and mix well.

2. To make the pastry, put the flour and icing sugar into a bowl, add the butter and rub in with your fingertips until it resembles fine breadcrumbs. Work in just enough water to bring the mixture together into a dough. Knead briefly until smooth, then wrap in cling film and leave to rest in the fridge for 30 minutes.

3. On a lightly floured surface, roll out the pastry to a 5mm thickness. Using a 10cm cutter, stamp out rounds. Place a generous tablespoonful of the currant mixture in the centre of each one. Brush the pastry edges with a little water, then gather them over the filling and press together to seal.

4. Turn the Chorley cakes over so the seal is underneath and roll each one gently with the rolling pin to flatten it slightly. Place on a baking tray lined with baking parchment and leave to rest in the fridge for 30 minutes. Heat the oven to 200°C/Gas 6.

5. Brush the Chorley cakes with a little milk. Sprinkle lightly with caster sugar and bake for 15–20 minutes, until golden brown. Let cool slightly. Dust with a little more sugar before serving.

PASTRY

275g plain flour
2 tbsp icing sugar
140g cold unsalted butter,
  cut into cubes
3–4 tbsp ice-cold water
A little milk, for brushing

FILLING

150g currants
75ml orange liqueur, such
  as Cointreau
50g caster sugar, plus extra
  for sprinkling
Grated zest of 1 orange

EQUIPMENT

A 10cm pastry cutter

RIPON SPICE CAKE

MAKES 1 LARGE OR 8 MINI TEA LOAVES

Dating back to Victorian times, this is the kind of lightly fruited cake you'll always find on a Yorkshire tea table. I've made it in mini loaf tins here – but of course you could stick with tradition and use a large tin, if you prefer.

100g unsalted butter, softened
200g caster sugar
1 large egg
225g plain flour
1 tsp baking powder
½ tsp ground mace
1 tsp ground mixed spice
25g ground almonds
70ml milk
50g glacé cherries, halved
100g currants
100g raisins
25g chopped mixed candied peel

EQUIPMENT

8 mini loaf tins or a 900g loaf tin

1. Heat the oven to 150°C/Gas 2. Lightly grease 8 mini loaf tins or a 900g loaf tin. If using a large loaf tin, line the base with baking parchment.

2. Beat the butter and sugar together until light and fluffy, then beat in the egg. Sift the flour, baking powder, mace and mixed spice together over the mixture and fold in, using a large metal spoon or spatula.

3. Now fold in the ground almonds, followed by the milk. Finally, stir in the dried fruit and candied peel.

4. Transfer the mixture to the prepared tins or tin and bake for 35 minutes for mini loaves or 1¼–1½ hours for a large loaf.

5. Leave in the tin(s) for 15 minutes, then transfer to a wire rack to cool.

6. Serve sliced with butter or with a small wedge of crumbly Wensleydale cheese.

YORKSHIRE PARKIN

MAKES 12 SQUARES

Guy Fawkes Night in Yorkshire just isn't the same without a thick slab of parkin to nibble on while you warm yourself by the bonfire. This dark, moist, treacly cake includes oatmeal, which makes it quite different from the many other British regional gingerbreads. Originally an ancient recipe, parkin was transformed by the addition of bicarbonate of soda. If you can manage to bake this a few days ahead, it will become stickier and richer as it matures.

1. Heat the oven to 170°C/Gas 3. Grease a 30 x 21cm baking tin with butter.

2. Put the butter, golden syrup and treacle in a pan and heat gently until melted. Beat the eggs with the milk in a jug.

3. Put the flour, bicarbonate of soda and ginger into a large bowl. Add the sugar and oatmeal and mix well. Stir in the melted butter and syrup mixture, followed by the eggs and milk.

4. Pour the mixture into the prepared baking tin and bake for 45–55 minutes, until the parkin has risen and springs back when pressed lightly with your finger. Don't worry if it sinks in the middle a little.

5. Leave to cool, then cut into squares. Store, wrapped in baking parchment, in an airtight tin.

225g unsalted butter
110g golden syrup
110g black treacle
2 large eggs
125ml milk
225g plain flour
1 tsp bicarbonate of soda
1 tbsp ground ginger
225g dark muscovado sugar
225g medium oatmeal

EQUIPMENT

A 30 x 21cm baking tin (or tin with similar dimensions)

CUMBRIAN SAND CAKE

MAKES A 20CM CAKE

Sand refers to the texture of this cake, which includes ground rice. I've added some ground almonds to soften the texture slightly and provide moisture. It's one of those slim, plain cakes that are very useful to have around as they keep for a good few days in an airtight tin. Originally it would have been served in small slices with a glass of sherry.

115g unsalted butter, softened
115g caster sugar
2 large eggs
Grated zest of 1 lemon
25g plain flour
1 tsp baking powder
90g ground rice
30g ground almonds
Icing sugar, for dusting

EQUIPMENT

A shallow 20cm round cake tin (such as a sandwich tin)

1. Heat the oven to 180°C/Gas 4. Grease a shallow 20cm round cake tin (such as a sandwich cake tin) and line the base with a disc of baking parchment.

2. Beat the butter and sugar together until very light and fluffy. Beat in the eggs one at a time, followed by the lemon zest.

3. Sift the flour, baking powder, ground rice and ground almonds together and fold them into the creamed mixture with a large metal spoon.

4. Transfer the mixture to the prepared tin and gently level the surface. Bake for 20–25 minutes, until the cake is golden brown and a skewer inserted in the centre comes out clean.

5. Leave the cake in the tin for 10 minutes, then turn out onto a wire rack to cool. Dust with icing sugar before serving.

GOOSNARGH CAKES

MAKES ABOUT 25

Not cakes but biscuits, these come from the village of Goosnargh in Lancashire. Rich and crumbly, like shortbread, they are delicately flavoured with caraway seeds. Caraway is a bit of a Marmite flavour: you either love it or hate it. Add a little at first, grinding the seeds with a pestle and mortar to give a more subtle flavour, if you like.

The dough for these biscuits is high in butter, so it can be quite difficult to handle. If you find the dough difficult to roll out, do it between two sheets of cling film or baking parchment, then peel off the top sheet to cut out the biscuits.

250g plain flour
200g cold unsalted butter, diced
1 tbsp caster sugar, plus extra
   for sprinkling
2 tsp caraway seeds
Icing sugar, for dusting

EQUIPMENT
A 6.5cm pastry cutter

1. Put the flour into a bowl, add the butter and rub it in until it resembles fine breadcrumbs. (If the butter becomes too soft while you're rubbing it in, just put the bowl in the fridge for a few minutes to firm it up again.) Stir in the sugar and caraway seeds and bring the mixture together to form a dough.

2. Wrap the dough in cling film and chill thoroughly in the fridge for about an hour.

3. Heat the oven to 180°C/Gas 4. Line a baking tray with baking parchment.

4. On a lightly floured surface, roll out the chilled dough to a 5mm thickness. Using a 6.5cm cutter, stamp out rounds and place on the prepared baking tray. Sprinkle generously with caster sugar.

5. Bake for 12–15 minutes until the biscuits just begin to colour slightly. Dust with icing sugar while still warm.

WALES

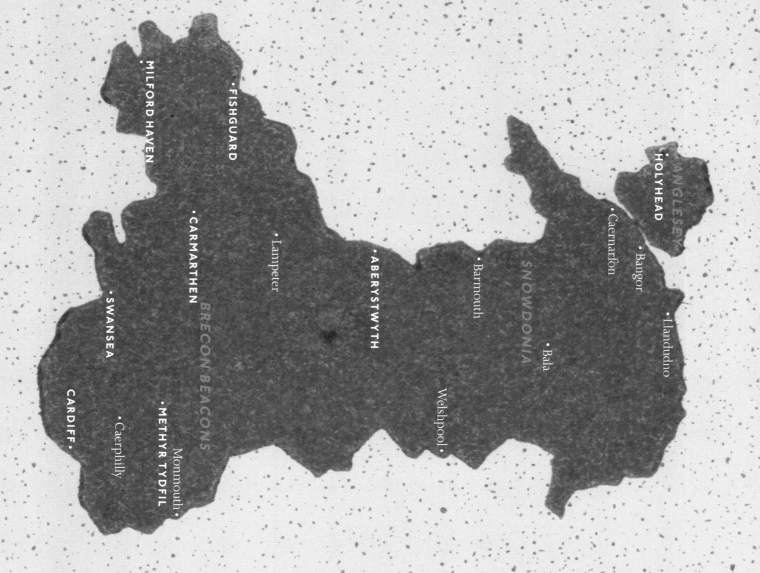

MILFORD HAVEN

FISHGUARD

HOLYHEAD

ANGLESEY

•Caernarfon

•Bangor

•Llandudno

CARMARTHEN

•Lampeter

ABERYSTWYTH

•Barmouth

SNOWDONIA

Welshpool•

•Bala

SWANSEA

BRECON BEACONS

CARDIFF•

•Caerphilly

METHYR TYDFIL

Monmouth•

Wales is predominantly farming country, with good soil, a relatively mild climate and a wealth of high-quality ingredients. There's the iconic leek, of course, but also lamb, shellfish, hedgerow fruits, dairy products and a surprisingly large collection of cheeses. All of these ingredients lend themselves to baking, whether pies and tarts, dairy-rich puddings such as Monmouth pudding (page 192), or simple cakes made with local honey and fresh fruit.

I love Caerphilly cheese and like to combine it with leeks in a tart (see page 186). The best-known cheese dish from Wales, Welsh rabbit (not rarebit, as it's often called) is usually made with English Cheddar because Welsh cheeses are too crumbly. It is said that Welshmen once bartered their sheep for Cheddar cheese – though since the rabbit is supposed to be a dish that arose out of poverty, I'm not convinced it would have been worth exchanging a sheep for.

They take teatime pretty seriously in Wales, though in the past cakes were strictly for Sundays. The famous bara brith (page 202) usually features, plus wholesome cakes such as honey buns (page 206) and a farmhouse cake (such as the one on page 212). It might not be fancy but it's as fine a spread as you'll get anywhere. The bakestone – or griddle – a round, flat, cast-iron slab, often with a hooped handle attached for suspending it over the hearth – still reigns supreme. It has given rise to some of the best-loved dishes of the region, including, of course, the Welsh cake (see page 199), whose Welsh name, *pice ar y maen*, means 'cooked on a stone'. Gently spiced and firmer than a drop scone, it has a character all of its own.

The bakestone was also traditionally used for pancakes, or *crempog*, bread, pies and oatcakes, which are thinner and crisper than the more familiar Scottish ones. Cooking a pie or a loaf of bread on the bakestone must have been quite an art. In the past, a cast-iron pot would have been upturned over it when baking bread to create a sort of mini oven. Little pies filled with jam or fruit are still sometimes cooked on an open griddle – a task that requires considerable skill.

I was born on St David's Day, so I have a bit of a soft spot for Wales. I do like Caerphilly cheese, so I've combined it with leeks here in order to fly the flag for Wales. Ingredients that are local to each other almost always taste good together and this is no exception.

PASTRY

200g plain flour
A pinch of salt
50g cold unsalted butter, diced
50g cold lard, diced
2–3 tbsp ice-cold water

FILLING

4 leeks, trimmed and well washed
25g butter, melted
2 medium eggs
125ml double cream
1 tbsp chopped parsley
1 tbsp thyme leaves
100g Caerphilly cheese, crumbled
Salt and pepper

EQUIPMENT

A 36 x 12cm loose-bottomed tart tin, 3cm deep (or a 23cm round tart tin)

STEP PHOTOGRAPHS OVERLEAF

1. To make the pastry, put the flour and salt in a large bowl and rub in the butter and lard with your fingertips until the mixture resembles fine breadcrumbs. Gradually mix in enough water to make a dough. Knead briefly until smooth, being careful not to overwork the dough, then wrap in cling film and chill for at least 30 minutes. Heat the oven to 200°C/Gas 6.

2. Roll out the pastry on a lightly floured surface to about a 3mm thickness and use to line a 36 x 12cm loose-bottomed tart tin, 3cm deep (or a 23cm round tin). Leave a little excess pastry overhanging the edge, and keep a small piece of pastry back in case you need to patch any cracks later.

3. Line the pastry case with baking parchment and fill with baking beans or dried beans or rice. Bake blind for 12–15 minutes, until the pastry is dry to the touch on the base. Carefully remove the parchment and beans and return the pastry case to the oven for about 5 minutes until it is very lightly coloured. Trim away the excess pastry from the edge. If there are any cracks or holes, use a tiny bit of the reserved raw pastry to patch them. Turn the oven down to 180°C/Gas 4.

4. Cut the leeks into even chunks, 2cm thick. Cook in a steamer for 6–8 minutes, until just tender, then remove and pat dry. Toss the leeks in the melted butter, being careful that they do not lose their shape. Season with salt and pepper and set aside.

5. Beat the eggs with the cream, herbs and some salt and pepper. Sprinkle half the cheese in the pastry case, arrange the leeks on top and pour on the creamy mixture. Scatter over the rest of the cheese. Bake for 20–25 minutes, until golden and just set. Leave in the tin for a few minutes before slicing. It's also good cold.

Lining the pastry case with baking parchment, ready to fill with baking beans to bake blind.

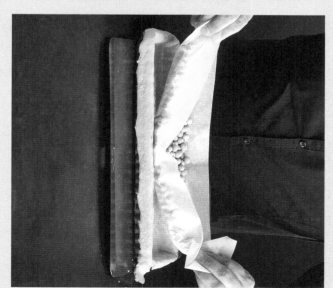

Carefully removing the paper and beans from the partially baked pastry case.

Beating together the eggs, cream, herbs and seasoning for the filling.

Arranging the buttery steamed leeks in the pastry case.

Carefully pouring the creamy mixture over the leeks in the pastry case before baking.

WELSH ONION CAKE

SERVES 4–6

This layered onion and potato cake makes a great accompaniment to lamb – Welsh lamb, of course, and if you can get wonderful salt-marsh lamb from Anglesea, then even better. Welsh mountain lamb is very tasty too, as the hardy sheep nibble on heather and herbs together with mountain grass.

1kg floury potatoes, such as
  Maris Piper
100g unsalted butter, melted
500g onions, thinly sliced
1 tbsp thyme leaves
Salt and pepper

EQUIPMENT

A 23–25cm ovenproof frying
  pan or shallow baking dish

1. Heat the oven to 200°C/Gas 6. Grease a 23–25cm ovenproof frying pan or shallow baking dish with butter and line the base with a disc of baking parchment.

2. Peel and thinly slice the potatoes. Put them into a bowl with the melted butter and some salt and pepper, and toss to coat.

3. Arrange a neat, overlapping layer of potatoes in the base of the frying pan or dish. Add a layer of onion and a little thyme. Repeat alternate layers of potato, onion and thyme, finishing with a neat layer of potatoes.

4. Cover with foil and bake for 50 minutes. Remove the foil and cook for a further 30 minutes, until the vegetables are tender and the top is crisp and golden brown. Turn out onto a plate, peel off the baking parchment and cut into wedges to serve.

I don't know why this pudding is named Monmouth in particular but it's an indulgent Welsh classic, with all the comfort factor of a suet pud yet none of the stodge. Fresh breadcrumbs cleverly stabilise the custard base. It's similar to queen of puddings, but with cooked fruit rather than jam. You could use stewed apples, pears, rhubarb or other fruit instead of plums, but make sure you boil off any juices, otherwise the mixture will be too wet.

600ml whole milk
1 vanilla pod
4 egg yolks
50g caster sugar
100g fresh white breadcrumbs

FRUIT LAYER
400g plums, pitted and cut into quarters
2 tbsp caster sugar
¼ tsp ground star anise

MERINGUE TOPPING
4 egg whites
100g caster sugar

EQUIPMENT
A 1.2–1.5 litre ovenproof dish

1. Heat the oven to 170°C/Gas 3. Lightly butter a 1.2–1.5 litre ovenproof dish.

2. Put the milk in a saucepan. Slit open the vanilla pod with a small, sharp knife and scrape out the seeds. Add the seeds and pod to the milk, heat until just boiling, then take off the heat.

3. Beat the egg yolks and sugar together in a bowl. Gradually pour on the hot milk, whisking as you do so. Strain into a jug.

4. Put the breadcrumbs in the prepared dish and pour the custard over them, making sure they are all moistened. Bake for about 20 minutes, until just set.

5. Meanwhile, put the plums, sugar and star anise into a saucepan, cover and cook gently until the plums are tender. Uncover the pan, turn up the heat a little and continue to cook for a few minutes until the mixture is thick and jammy.

6. For the meringue, whisk the egg whites with an electric whisk until they hold stiff peaks. Add the sugar, a spoonful at a time, continuing to whisk until you have a fluffy meringue that holds stiff peaks. Increase the oven setting to 180°C/Gas 4.

7. Spread the cooked plums over the custard base, then spoon the meringue over them, pulling up the top into peaks with a round-bladed knife, if you like.

8. Return the pudding to the oven and bake for 10–15 minutes, until the meringue is golden. Leave to settle for 5–10 minutes, then serve.

CRUSTY SWANSEA

MAKES 1 LARGE LOAF

To most of us this is a large white bloomer, but to the people of South Wales it's a crusty Swansea. Essentially, it's a light, airy loaf with a chewy golden crust, slashed before baking in a steamy oven to make it even crustier. I've gone for the traditional elongated shape here but you can also make it into a round loaf.

500g strong white bread flour
7g salt
7g sachet instant yeast
30g unsalted butter, diced and softened
320ml water

STEP PHOTOGRAPHS OVERLEAF

1. Put the flour in a large bowl. Add the salt on one side, the yeast on the other. Add the butter and three-quarters of the water and turn the mix with the fingers of one hand. Add the remaining water a little at a time, mixing until all the flour is taken in and you have a soft, rough dough; you might not need all the water.

2. Oil the work surface to prevent sticking. Turn out the dough and knead for at least 5 minutes, until smooth and silky. Lightly oil the bowl, return the dough to it and cover with cling film. Leave to rise for at least an hour, until tripled in size.

3. Line a baking tray with baking parchment. Scrape the dough out onto a lightly floured surface and fold it inwards repeatedly until all the air is knocked out and it is smooth.

4. To shape, flatten into a rectangle with a long side facing you. Fold each end into the middle, then roll it up so you have a smooth top with a seam underneath. Very gently roll with the heels of your hands to improve the shape.

5. Lift the loaf onto the prepared tray, put in a clean plastic bag and leave to prove for about an hour, until doubled in size. Heat the oven to 220°C/Gas Mark 7.

6. Place a baking tray containing water on the bottom shelf of the oven. Lightly spray the top of the loaf with water and dust with flour. Make 3–5 diagonal slashes across the top.

7. Bake the loaf on the middle shelf of the oven for 25 minutes. Lower the setting to 200°C/Gas Mark 6 and bake for a further 10 minutes, until the loaf is golden brown on top and sounds hollow when tapped underneath. Cool on a wire rack.

Coating the work surface with a little oil to prevent the dough sticking during kneading.

Starting the kneading action by first pushing the top of the dough away from you.

Continuing the kneading action by bringing the stretched top of the dough back in and tucking it into the middle.

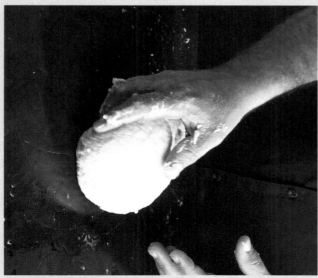

Turning the dough 45° before repeating the kneading action over and over again until the dough is smooth and pliable.

Lifting the risen dough out of the bowl onto a lightly floured surface.

Folding the dough inwards and punching it down to knock out the air.

The formed loaf, gently rolled with the heels of the hands to improve the shape, ready to be transferred to the baking tray for proving.

Making several evenly spaced slashes, on the diagonal, across the top of the proved loaf before baking.

WELSH CAKES

MAKES 18–20

You can add all sorts of flavours to these to bling them up but a good old Welsh cake with just a bit of butter is perfect for me. In the great tradition of Celtic baking, they are cooked on a cast-iron pan rather than in the oven. If you don't have a flat griddle pan, any large, heavy-based frying pan will do. A thick base is important for even heat distribution and to help prevent the scones burning. Keep the heat fairly low, so the Welsh cakes cook through to the centre without becoming too dark on the outside.

1. Sift the flour, baking powder and mixed spice into a bowl. Add the butter and rub it in with your fingertips until the mixture resembles fine breadcrumbs. Stir in the sugar and currants, mix in the egg, then add enough milk to form a firm dough.

2. On a lightly floured surface, roll out the scone dough to a 5mm thickness. Stamp out rounds using a 7.5cm fluted cutter, re-rolling the trimmings to cut more as necessary.

3. Place a flat griddle or a large heavy-based frying pan over a low-medium heat. When it is hot, grease it with a little butter or oil. Cook the Welsh cakes, in batches, for 3–4 minutes on each side, adjusting the heat if necessary so they are golden brown on the outside and cooked right through.

4. Remove the Welsh cakes from the griddle and sprinkle with caster sugar. They are best served immediately – though any left over will also be good cold, or heated gently in a toaster or under the grill the next day.

265g plain flour
1½ tsp baking powder
½ tsp ground mixed spice
130g unsalted butter, diced
90g caster sugar, plus extra
   for sprinkling
75g currants
1 medium or large egg,
   lightly beaten
1–2 tbsp milk

EQUIPMENT

A flat griddle (or large heavy-
   based frying pan)
A 7.5cm fluted pastry cutter

STEP PHOTOGRAPHS OVERLEAF

Rolling out the dough to a 5mm thickness on a lightly floured surface.

Cutting out rounds using a 7.5cm fluted cutter and transferring them to a tray, ready to cook on the griddle.

BARA BRITH

MAKES 1 LARGE TEA LOAF

Bara brith means speckled bread, a reassuringly homely name for this delicious teabread. There is also a yeasted version, which is similar to the Irish barm brack on page 238. The speckling comes from dried fruit, but I've included some fresh fruit too, which makes it beautifully moist. If you'd like to try the classic bara brith, replace the apple and plums with 125g mixed raisins and currants.

1. Place the sultanas in a bowl and pour the hot tea over them. Cover and leave to soak overnight.

2. The next day, heat the oven to 150°C/Gas 2. Grease a 1kg loaf tin and line it with baking parchment.

3. Peel the cooking apple, grate half of it and cut the other half into small pieces. Add all the apple to the soaked fruit and tea, together with all the remaining ingredients, and mix well.

4. Tip the mixture into the prepared tin, gently smooth the top and bake for about 1½ hours, until a skewer inserted in the centre comes out clean.

5. Leave in the tin for 10 minutes, then turn out onto a wire rack to cool. Serve sliced and buttered.

300g sultanas

300ml hot, strong black tea

1 cooking apple

2 plums, pitted and finely chopped

50g dark muscovado sugar

250g self-raising flour

50g ground almonds

2 medium eggs

EQUIPMENT

A 1kg loaf tin

WELSH GINGERBREAD

MAKES 12 SQUARES

Strangely enough, many old recipes for Welsh gingerbread don't include any ginger. It seems to have been a general name for cakes sold at festivals and fairs. I've added ginger here, but you could leave it out if you like. It's kidology – the black treacle adds lots of flavour and tricks you into thinking the cake contains ginger.

It's worth buying the large pieces of candied peel that you cut yourself for this. They have much more flavour than ready-chopped candied peel and it really makes a difference to the end result.

1. Heat the oven to 170°C/Gas 3. Grease and line a 27 x 20cm baking tin (or tin with similar dimensions).

2. Sift the flour into a large bowl with the ginger, if using. Add the butter and rub it in with your fingertips until the mixture resembles fine breadcrumbs. Stir in the sugar and candied peel.

3. Put the treacle, honey and milk in a saucepan and heat gently, stirring, until the treacle and honey have melted into the milk. Pour onto the dry ingredients and mix thoroughly.

4. Pour the mixture into the prepared baking tin and bake for 30–40 minutes, until a skewer inserted in the centre comes out clean.

5. Leave to cool completely, then cut into squares. Store in an airtight tin. The gingerbread will mature and become stickier with keeping.

350g self-raising flour
3 tsp ground ginger (optional)
100g unsalted butter, diced
150g demerara sugar
50g mixed candied peel, chopped
50g black treacle
80g honey
150ml milk

EQUIPMENT

A 27 x 20cm baking tin (or tin with similar dimensions)

HONEY BUNS

Honey seems to have been used for sweetening cakes in Wales long after it was replaced by sugar elsewhere. There are some excellent local honey producers and buying a well-flavoured honey will really enhance these little buns. I have added pecan nuts and a cream cheese icing to bring them bang up to date.

200g plain flour

½ tsp bicarbonate of soda

1 tsp ground cinnamon

100g unsalted butter, softened

100g light soft brown sugar

1 large egg, separated

100g honey

1–2 tbsp milk (if needed)

75g pecan nuts, chopped

ICING

75g full-fat cream cheese

100g icing sugar

2 tbsp runny honey

18 pecan nuts, to decorate

EQUIPMENT

Two 12-hole bun trays

STEP PHOTOGRAPHS
OVERLEAF

1. Heat the oven to 200°C/Gas 6. Line two 12-hole bun trays with 18 fairy cake cases.

2. Sift the flour, bicarbonate of soda and cinnamon into a bowl and set aside.

3. In another bowl, beat the butter and sugar together until light and fluffy, then beat in the egg yolk, followed by the honey. Fold in the flour mixture using a large metal spoon or spatula, adding a little milk, if necessary, to give a stiff batter. Add the pecan nuts and mix well.

4. Whisk the egg white in a separate bowl until stiff and fold it into the mixture.

5. Divide the mixture between the paper cases. Bake for about 15 minutes, until the cakes are well risen and golden brown. Transfer to a wire rack to cool.

6. To make the icing, put the cream cheese into a bowl and beat in the icing sugar until smooth. Stir in the honey.

7. Spread the icing on top of each honey bun with a palette knife and decorate with a pecan nut.

Beating the butter and soft brown sugar together until smooth and creamy.

Beating in the egg yolk, followed by the honey.

Folding the flour mixture in, using a large metal spoon.

Spooning the cake mixture into the fairy cases in the bun tray.

Spreading the icing on top of the buns with a small palette knife.

WHITE CHOCOLATE AND CHERRY PLATE CAKE

MAKES A 20CM CAKE

My nan was Welsh and she used to make a lot of plate pies. She had an ancient set of enamel plates, which she used for everything. It's worth investing in some – unbreakable, they last for ever. Purists might be shocked by my contemporary treatment of the much-loved Welsh plate cake (*teisen lap*), but I'm convinced they will be won round when they taste it. This buttery, crumbly cake usually includes currants and raisins. Replacing them with white chocolate and dried cherries lifts it to a new level of gorgeousness.

225g plain flour
A pinch of salt
2 tsp baking powder
A little freshly grated nutmeg
110g unsalted butter, diced
110g caster sugar
100g dried cherries
100g white chocolate drops
2 medium or large eggs, lightly beaten
About 100ml milk
A little demerara sugar, for sprinkling

EQUIPMENT

A 20cm enamel or metal pie plate

1. Heat the oven to 180°C/Gas 4. Grease a 20cm enamel or metal pie plate with butter.

2. Sift the flour, salt and baking powder into a bowl and grate in the nutmeg. Rub in the butter with your fingertips until the mixture resembles fine breadcrumbs.

3. Stir in the sugar, followed by the cherries and chocolate. Mix in the eggs and enough milk to give a consistency that is just soft enough for the mixture to drop from the spoon.

4. Spoon the mixture onto the greased pie plate and spread evenly. Sprinkle over a little demerara sugar. Bake for about 30 minutes, until golden brown and firm to the touch and a skewer inserted in the centre comes out clean.

5. Allow to cool slightly before serving. This cake is best eaten slightly warm.

FARMHOUSE WALNUT CAKE

MAKES A 20CM CAKE

A lovely iced vanilla sponge with a nutty texture that was originally made for special teas and celebrations. Traditionally it would have been a round cake, sandwiched together with the icing, but I think it works equally well as a traybake.

200g unsalted butter, softened
150g caster sugar
2 large eggs
200g self-raising flour
¼ tsp vanilla extract
50g walnut halves, chopped, plus extra to decorate

BUTTERCREAM

80g unsalted butter, softened
160g icing sugar
¼ tsp vanilla extract
2–3 tsp milk

EQUIPMENT

A shallow 20cm square cake tin

1. Heat the oven to 180°C/Gas 4. Grease and line a shallow 20cm square cake tin.

2. Beat the butter and sugar together until light and fluffy. Beat in the eggs one at a time, adding 1 tbsp of the flour with the last one, then beat in the vanilla. Sift the remaining flour over the mixture and fold it in with a large metal spoon. Finally, fold in the chopped walnuts.

3. Transfer the mixture to the prepared tin and level the surface. Bake for 20–25 minutes, until risen and golden brown. Leave the cake in the tin for 5 minutes, then turn out onto a wire rack and leave to cool completely.

4. To make the buttercream, beat the butter in a bowl until very soft. Add the icing sugar and beat until smooth. Beat in the vanilla extract and enough milk to give a spreadable consistency.

5. Spread the icing on top of the cooled cake with a palette knife and decorate with the walnut halves.

IRELAND

Dingle

COUNTY KERRY

COUNTY LIMERICK

•CORK

•WATERFORD

•KILKENNY

Wexford•

•GALWAY

ÉIRE

•Athlone

•Castlebar

•Sligo

DUBLIN•

•DONEGAL

•Omagh

DERRY

NORTHERN
IRELAND

Larne
•

BELFAST

Oats, wheat, milk and potatoes have formed the backbone of Irish cooking for centuries. These four staples are undoubtedly humble but the genius of Irish cooks lies in their ability to take simple ingredients and create something outstanding with them. Nowhere is this more evident than in their baking.

Bread is the heart and soul of Irish cooking and there is a large range of loaves, scones, pancakes and other baked goods, based not just on oats and wheat but also on potatoes. These are so good that they are virtually a meal in themselves: think of a stack of oatmeal drop scones straight from the pan, or a farl of soft, warm potato bread, or even a slice or two of the moist, crumbly soda bread for which Ireland is justly famous. Slather any of these with salted butter, tuck in a rasher of bacon or a sausage and you have a feast.

One of the great things about these breads is that they are ideal for the novice baker. There's no yeast to handle for most of them. They rely on bicarbonate of soda for their rise, often used in combination with buttermilk, whose acidity gives the soda a kick-start. It takes just minutes to mix the ingredients and, because there is no lengthy rising, you can get a loaf on the table within an hour. If you bake on a griddle, as so many Irish recipes call for, you can produce all sorts of pancakes and drop scones, made with little more than flour or oatmeal, potato and a generous slosh of buttermilk.

The traditional diet may be simple but there is a generosity about it, particularly when it comes to celebrations. The Irish are renowned for their hospitality – is it any wonder when you think of the convivial effects of their two most famous exports, whiskey and Guinness? These are great, not only for drinking but for cooking with too.

Guinness has been used for generations to enrich stews and other meat dishes but it's also a brilliant addition to cakes, such as the porter cake on page 247 and the non-traditional Guinness and black muffins (page 244). Just about any dish is improved with the addition of a little (or even a lot of) whiskey. One of the great modern classics is the Irish coffee cake (page 241), which takes all the elements of the drink of the same name and reinvents them in cake form. Now that's ingenious.

DINGLE LAMB PIE

SERVES 4–6

Dingle, in County Kerry, is sheep-rearing country and famous for its pies, which were baked for fairs and saints' days. Scraps of mutton and vegetables often found their way into pocket-sized pies, for fishermen and farmers to take to work. This hearty plate pie makes a little meat go a long way; it's good hot or cold.

1. For the pastry, mix the flour and salt together in a large bowl and rub in the butter and lard with your fingertips until the mixture resembles fine breadcrumbs. Mix in enough water to form a firm dough and knead briefly until smooth. Wrap in cling film and chill while you make the filling.

2. For the filling, heat 1 tbsp of the oil in a wide, heavy-based pan (that has a lid), add the onion, carrot and potato with a pinch of salt, and cook gently for 5–6 minutes, until starting to soften but not colour. Remove to a plate with a slotted spoon.

3. Heat the remaining oil in the pan, add the lamb and brown on all sides over a fairly high heat. Lower the heat, stir in the flour and cook for a minute, then gradually stir in the stock. Return the vegetables to the pan and add the thyme, Worcestershire sauce and some salt and pepper. Cover and simmer gently for 30–40 minutes, until the meat is tender. Leave to cool.

4. Heat the oven to 200°C/Gas 6. Cut off about a third of the pastry and set aside for the lid. Roll out the rest on a lightly floured surface to about a 3mm thickness and use to line a 24cm pie plate. Roll out the other piece of pastry to form a lid.

5. Spoon the lamb filling onto the pastry-lined plate. Brush the pastry edges with a little beaten egg, then position the lid over the filling and trim off the excess pastry around the rim.

6. Crimp the pastry edges to seal and make 3 small slits in the middle of the pie to let steam out. Brush the top with more beaten egg, then bake for 30–35 minutes, until golden brown. Leave to stand for 15 minutes before serving. This pie is good hot or cold.

PASTRY

300g plain flour
A pinch of salt
75g cold unsalted butter, diced
75g cold lard, diced
About 4 tbsp ice-cold water
1 egg, lightly beaten, to glaze

FILLING

2 tbsp sunflower oil
1 large onion, finely chopped
1 carrot, finely chopped
1 medium potato, peeled and
    cut into small dice
300g lamb shoulder, cut into
    1–2cm pieces
1 tbsp plain flour
300ml lamb stock
2–3 sprigs of thyme
A splash of Worcestershire
    sauce
Salt and pepper

EQUIPMENT

A 24cm pie plate

STEP PHOTOGRAPHS
OVERLEAF

Spooning the lamb and vegetable filling into the pastry case.

Lifting the rolled-out larger (two-thirds) portion of pastry onto the enamel pie plate.

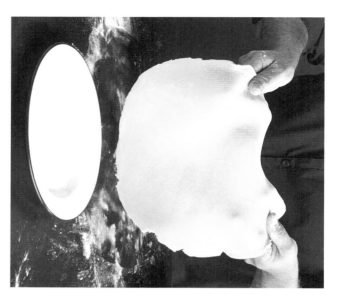

Brushing the pastry on the rim of the pie plate with a little beaten egg.

Gently pressing the pastry onto the base and sides and into the corners of the pie plate.

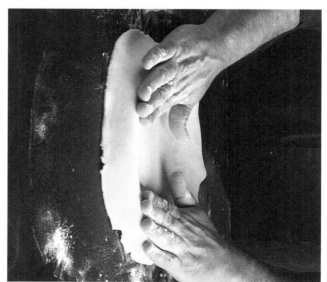

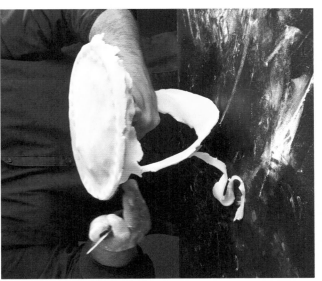

Cutting away the excess pastry overhanging the edge of the pie plate, using a small, sharp knife.

Making 3 small slits in the middle of the pastry lid, to allow steam to escape during baking.

Positioning the pastry lid over the pie filling.

Crimping the edges of the pastry between the thumb and forefingers to seal the pie and create a decorative edge.

SERVES 6

This gently spiced pudding, traditionally eaten at Halloween, is like a simpler version of Christmas pudding, but made with buttermilk to give a light, moist texture. Serve with brandy custard or ice cream – or both, of course!

55g plain flour
55g caster sugar
80g cold unsalted butter, diced
½ tsp bicarbonate of soda
½ tsp freshly grated nutmeg
½ tsp ground cinnamon
¼ tsp ground cloves
½ tsp salt
225g mixed dried fruit
100g brown breadcrumbs
1 tbsp golden syrup
150–175ml buttermilk

EQUIPMENT
A 1.2 litre pudding basin

1. Generously butter a 1.2 litre pudding basin and line the base with a disc of baking parchment.

2. Put the flour and sugar into a bowl, add the butter and rub it in with your fingertips. Add all the remaining ingredients except the buttermilk and mix thoroughly. Gradually stir in enough buttermilk to form a soft mixture. Spoon the mixture into the prepared basin.

3. Place a piece of baking parchment over a sheet of foil and make a large pleat in the middle, folding both sheets together (this allows the pudding to expand as it cooks). Put the parchment and foil on top of the pudding basin, foil-side up, and secure with string, looping the end of the string over the top of the pudding and tying it to form a handle that will enable you to lift the pudding in and out of the saucepan.

4. Stand the pudding basin in a large steamer. Cover and steam for 2½ hours, topping up the boiling water if necessary so it doesn't boil dry. (If you don't have a steamer, stand the basin in a large saucepan and pour in enough boiling water to come halfway up the side of the basin, then put the lid on the pan and simmer for 2½ hours, topping up the water as necessary.)

5. Remove the pudding basin from the pan and take off the foil and parchment. Invert a large plate over the top of the basin and then turn both over to unmould the pudding.

BOXTY PANCAKES

MAKES ABOUT 20

Boxty on the griddle, boxty on the pan,
If you can't make boxty, you'll never get a man.

Well, never fear, this is how you make boxty. I have eaten these potato pancakes in Ireland and they're fantastic. They rely on a mixture of mashed potato and grated raw potato for their unique texture. I'd have them with bacon any day of the week, or as part of an Ulster fry – the Irish equivalent of a full English.

1. Coarsely grate the peeled raw potato into a bowl, then add the mashed potato. Add the flour, salt and bicarbonate of soda and mix thoroughly. Gradually stir in enough buttermilk to form a thick batter.

2. You'll need to cook the pancakes in batches. Heat a flat griddle or a large heavy-based frying pan over a medium-high heat. Add a little butter or oil and swirl it round the pan.

3. When the griddle is hot, add 2 tbsp of the batter for each pancake, spreading it roughly into a round using the back of the spoon. Cook for 2–3 minutes, until golden underneath and beginning to set on top – small holes will appear on the surface of the pancake at this stage. Turn over and cook the other side for a minute or so, until lightly coloured.

4. Eat straight away, or keep warm in a low oven while you fry the remaining mixture.

125g floury potato, such as King Edward or Maris Piper, peeled
125g cold mashed potato
125g plain flour
½ tsp salt
¼ tsp bicarbonate of soda
About 250ml buttermilk
A little butter or oil for frying

EQUIPMENT
A flat griddle (or large heavy-based frying pan)

STEP PHOTOGRAPHS
OVERLEAF

Coarsely grating the raw potato into a large bowl, before adding the mashed potato, flour, salt and bicarbonate of soda.

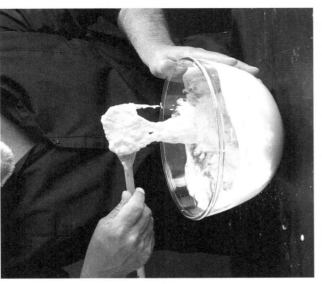

Gradually stirring in the buttermilk, keeping the mixture free from lumps.

Checking the consistency of the pancake batter: it should be smooth and thick.

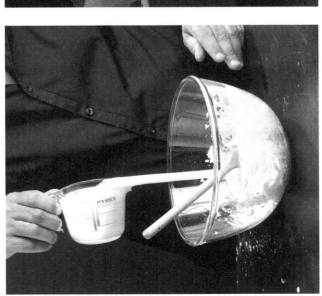

Spooning 2 tbsp of the batter onto the greased, hot griddle and spreading it into a round with the back of the spoon.

Turning the pancake over when the top is starting to set and it is peppered with small holes, using a palette knife.

OATMEAL DROP SCONES

150g fine oatmeal
400ml buttermilk
75g self-raising flour
1 tsp bicarbonate of soda
2 tbsp runny honey
1 medium egg, lightly beaten
50ml milk
A little vegetable oil for frying

EQUIPMENT

A flat griddle (or large heavy-based frying pan)

I love cooking drop scones on a griddle. Try these for breakfast, as a change from porridge. As long as you remember to soak the oatmeal in the buttermilk the night before, you can have them ready very quickly. Just don't cook them at too high a heat, or the outside will burn before the centre is cooked through.

1. Mix the oatmeal with the buttermilk and leave to soak for a few hours or overnight.

2. Add the flour and bicarbonate of soda to the oatmeal mixture and stir until thoroughly combined. Mix in the honey and egg, then add enough milk to make a batter the consistency of double cream.

3. You'll need to cook the drop scones in batches. Grease a flat griddle or a large heavy-based frying pan with a little oil and place over a medium-low heat.

4. When it is hot, drop spoonfuls of the batter onto the griddle, leaving enough room for them to spread and find their own level. Cook for 2–3 minutes, until bubbles appear on the surface and they are beginning to dry out around the edge, then turn them over and cook the other side.

5. Serve hot from the pan, with butter, honey, syrup or jam.

SODA BREAD

MAKES 1 SMALL LOAF

250g plain white flour
250g plain wholemeal flour
1 tsp salt
1 tsp bicarbonate of soda
About 400ml buttermilk

STEP PHOTOGRAPHS
OVERLEAF

Ireland's most famous bread is made with two of its oldest foods, wheat and buttermilk. The acid in the buttermilk reacts with the bicarbonate of soda and creates the rise. If you have kids, do teach them how to make soda bread, because it's great to be able to put a loaf on the table within 45 minutes. Once you've mastered it, try adding some grated Wexford cheese (vintage Irish Cheddar) and chopped raw onion to the dough.

1. Heat the oven to 200°C/Gas 6. Line a baking tray with baking parchment.

2. Put the flours, salt and bicarbonate of soda into a large bowl and mix well. Make a well in the centre and pour in half the buttermilk. Using your fingers or a round-bladed knife, draw the flour into the buttermilk. Continue to add the buttermilk until all the flour has been absorbed and you have a sticky dough. You may not need all the buttermilk – it depends on the flour you use.

3. Tip the dough out on to a lightly floured surface, shape it into a ball and flatten it slightly with the palm of your hand. It is important to work quickly, as once the buttermilk is added it begins to react with the bicarbonate of soda.

4. Put the dough on the baking tray. Mark into quarters with a large, sharp knife, cutting deeply through the loaf, almost but not quite through to the base. Dust the top with flour.

5. Bake for 30 minutes or until the loaf is golden brown and sounds hollow when tapped on the base. Leave to cool on a wire rack. Eat on the day of baking – or toast it the next day.

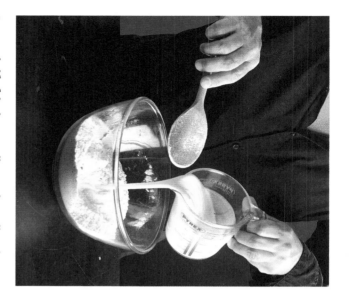

Pouring half of the buttermilk into the well in the centre of the dry ingredients.

Bringing the mixture together, having added enough buttermilk to form a sticky dough.

Shaping the dough into a smooth, round ball on a lightly floured surface.

Flattening the ball of dough slightly with the palm of the hand.

Marking the dough into quarters, cutting deeply with a large, sharp knife, almost but not quite right through to the base.

OAT BREAD

MAKES 1 SMALL LOAF

Oats have been cultivated in Ireland for centuries and oat mills are still flourishing to this day. Oats are highly nutritious, so if you're not a fan of porridge you can get your daily dose in this bread. Like so many Irish loaves, this one is yeast-free and quick to make. I enjoy it toasted, for breakfast or tea, with a little butter or cheese.

75g self-raising flour
50g wholemeal self-raising flour
1 tsp salt
50g unsalted butter, diced
1 tbsp dark soft brown sugar
100g fine oatmeal
200–250ml buttermilk

EQUIPMENT
A 500g loaf tin

1. Heat the oven to 200°C/Gas 6. Grease a 500g loaf tin and line it with baking parchment.

2. Mix the flours and salt together in a bowl, then rub in the butter with your fingertips until the mixture resembles fine breadcrumbs. Stir in the sugar and oatmeal, then mix in enough buttermilk to form a wet paste.

3. Transfer the mixture to the prepared tin and smooth the surface. Bake for about 45 minutes, until the loaf has a golden crust and sounds hollow when tapped on the base. Leave to cool on a wire rack.

BOXTY BREAD

MAKES 1 SMALL LOAF

Boxty bread is often made on a griddle and cut into quarters or farls before cooking, but some versions, like this one, are baked in the oven. Potato brings a lot to the party. The extra starch it provides makes a fantastically moist, well-flavoured loaf and also improves its keeping qualities. Great with a traditional fry-up, boxty bread is best eaten still warm from the oven, spread with generous amounts of salted butter.

200g floury potatoes, such as
    King Edward or Maris Piper,
    peeled
200g mashed potato
200g self-raising flour
1 tsp salt
30g lard, melted
About 75ml milk

1. Heat the oven to 200°C/Gas 6. Line a baking tray with baking parchment.

2. Coarsely grate the peeled potatoes onto a clean tea towel. Gather the grated potato up in the tea towel and wring it out over the sink to extract as much liquid as possible.

3. Mix the grated and mashed potato together in a bowl. Add the flour and salt and combine well. Stir in the melted lard, then add enough milk to form a soft dough.

4. Turn the dough out onto a lightly floured surface and knead briefly until smooth. Shape into a round and place on the prepared baking tray.

5. Mark the loaf into quarters with a large, sharp knife, cutting deeply, almost but not quite through to the base. Dust the top with flour.

6. Bake for 40 minutes, until risen and golden brown. Transfer the loaf to a wire rack to cool. To serve, break into quarters and eat warm or cold.

Like the Welsh bara brith (see page 202), this translates as speckled bread. One of the best fruited loaves around, it's traditionally served at Halloween with clues to the year ahead hidden inside: a coin in your slice signifies good fortune; a ring suggests a wedding; the stick an unhappy marriage; while a pea or a thimble means you're doomed to stay single for the coming year.

200g mixed dried fruit
250ml hot, strong black tea
350g strong white bread flour
1 tsp salt
1 tsp instant yeast
25g unsalted butter, softened
1 tbsp light soft brown sugar
1 large egg
80ml warm milk
About 50ml water
½ tsp ground cinnamon
½ tsp ground mixed spice

1. Place the dried fruit in a bowl, pour over the hot tea and leave to soak overnight.

2. The next day, put the flour into a free-standing electric mixer fitted with a dough hook. Add the salt to one side of the bowl, the yeast to the other. Add the butter, sugar, egg, milk and half the water and begin mixing on a slow speed. As the dough starts to come together, slowly add enough of the remaining water to give a soft dough; you might not need all the water.

3. Mix on a medium speed for 5 minutes; the dough should be soft and elastic but not wet or sticky. If it looks unmixed or breaks easily when you tug it, mix for 2 minutes longer.

4. Drain the dried fruit very thoroughly and add to the mixer with the ground spices. Mix on a low speed for 2 minutes.

5. Remove the dough hook and cover the bowl with cling film. Leave the dough to rise for 2–3 hours, until it has doubled in size. Line a baking tray with baking parchment.

6. Scrape the dough out onto a lightly floured surface and fold it inwards repeatedly until all the air is knocked out and the dough is smooth.

7. Shape into a ball and place on the prepared baking tray. Put the tray into a clean plastic bag and leave to prove for 1 hour or until the loaf has doubled in size. Heat the oven to 220°C/Gas 7.

8. Bake the loaf for 20–25 minutes, until it is golden brown and sounds hollow when tapped underneath. Leave to cool on a wire rack. Serve sliced and buttered.

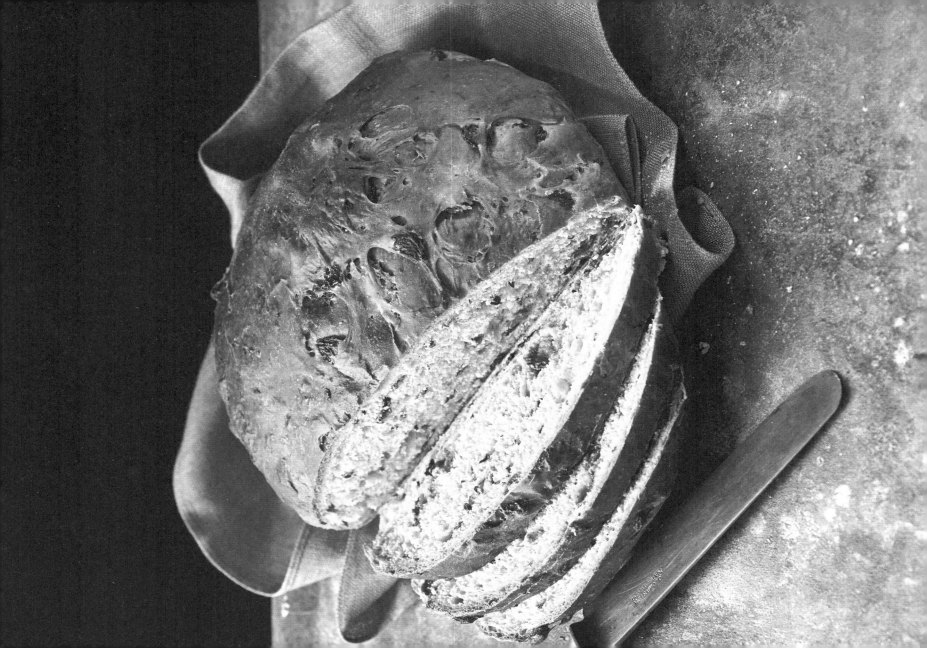

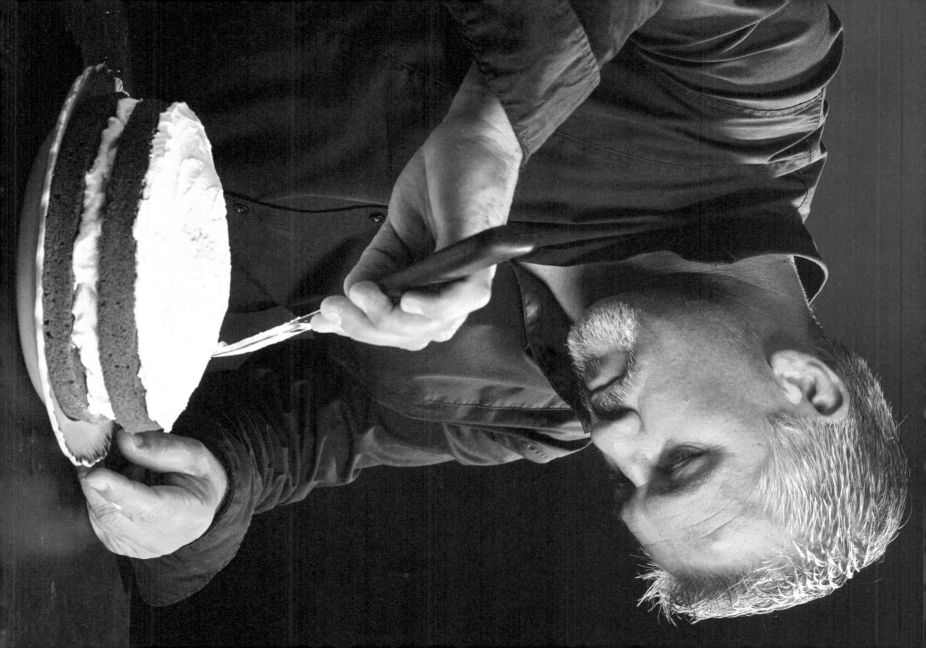

IRISH COFFEE CAKE

MAKES A 20CM CAKE

Irish coffee was invented in County Limerick in 1943 by chef Joe Sheridan, to cheer up a group of Americans who had just arrived by flying boat on a stormy night. The drink was a huge success and since then the famous coffee, cream and Irish whiskey medley has found its way into various recipes. Here a light coffee and chocolate sponge is saturated in a coffee and whiskey syrup and topped with whiskey-flavoured cream. Think of it as an Irish tiramisu.

175g unsalted butter, softened
175g caster sugar
3 large eggs
200g self-raising flour
20g cocoa powder, plus extra
  for dusting
4 tsp instant espresso powder
1 tsp vanilla extract
60ml hot water

SYRUP
75ml strong black coffee
75g caster sugar
40ml Irish whiskey

FILLING
300ml double cream
2 tbsp icing sugar
1 tbsp Irish whiskey

EQUIPMENT
Two 20cm sandwich cake tins

STEP PHOTOGRAPHS
OVERLEAF

1. Heat the oven to 180°C/Gas 4. Grease two 20cm sandwich cake tins and line the bases with baking parchment.

2. Put the butter and sugar in a bowl and beat together until light and fluffy. Beat in the eggs one at a time, adding a spoonful of the flour with the last one if it threatens to curdle.

3. Sift the remaining flour and the cocoa powder over the surface of the mixture and then fold in, using a large metal spoon or spatula. Mix the espresso powder, vanilla extract and hot water together and fold in.

4. Divide the mixture between the cake tins and level the surface. Bake for 25–30 minutes, until the cakes are well risen and spring back when pressed lightly with your finger. Leave in the tins for 5 minutes, then turn out and cool on a wire rack.

5. To make the syrup, put the coffee in a small pan, add the sugar and bring to the boil, stirring to dissolve the sugar. Take off the heat and stir in the whiskey.

6. When the cakes are cool, invert one onto a serving plate and place the other on a board, upside down. Using a pastry brush, brush them liberally with the coffee and whiskey syrup to soak.

7. For the filling, whisk the cream with the icing sugar to soft peaks, then fold in the whiskey. Spread half the cream over the cake on the plate. Invert the other cake on top and spread the top with the remaining cream. Dust with a little cocoa powder.

Folding the espresso and vanilla liquid into the cake mixture.

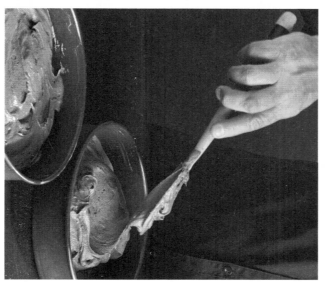

Dividing the cake mixture between the prepared sandwich tins.

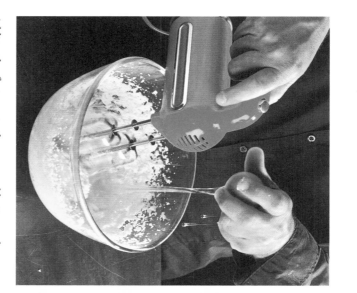

Adding the first egg to the creamed butter and sugar mixture.

Carefully folding the flour and cocoa into the mixture, using a spatula, trying to retain the air incorporated during whisking.

Brushing the top cake layer liberally with the coffee and whiskey mixture.

Checking whether the cake layer is cooked by pressing lightly with the fingers – the cake should spring back.

Sandwiching the cake layers together with half of the whiskey cream filling.

Adding the whiskey to the sweetened cream for the filling.

Not an original Irish recipe but I reckon it deserves to become a classic. Beer connoisseurs might disapprove of putting blackcurrant cordial in a pint of Guinness, but combine the two in a muffin with chocolate chips? Now you're talking. Use whatever chocolate you like – it's not always necessary to go the high cocoa solids route. It's more important to choose one you like. I'll leave you with the dilemma of what to do with the rest of the Guinness bottle...

65g unsalted butter, softened
140g dark muscovado sugar
1 large egg
100g plain flour
1 tbsp cocoa powder
¼ tsp bicarbonate of soda
¼ tsp baking powder
20ml Ribena or other
   blackcurrant cordial
50g dark chocolate chips
50ml Guinness

TOPPING
125g mascarpone cheese
65g icing sugar

EQUIPMENT
A 24-hole mini muffin tray

1. Heat the oven to 180°C/Gas 4. Grease a 24-hole mini muffin tray with butter.

2. Put the butter and sugar into a bowl and beat with a handheld electric whisk until soft and fluffy. Beat in the egg until evenly combined.

3. Add the flour, cocoa powder, bicarbonate of soda and baking powder and beat briefly until well incorporated. Now add the blackcurrant cordial and chocolate chips and mix well. Finally, stir in the Guinness.

4. Divide the mixture between the mini muffin moulds and bake for 12–15 minutes, until the muffins are well risen and a skewer inserted in the centre comes out clean. Leave to cool in the tin for 5 minutes, then run a knife around the edge of each one and turn out onto a wire rack to cool completely.

5. For the topping, beat the mascarpone and icing sugar together in a bowl with a wooden spoon until smooth. Spread on top of the muffins with a small palette knife.

PORTER CAKE

MAKES A 20CM CAKE

Porter is a type of stout; in fact 'stout porter' was the Victorian name for strong porter, later shortened to stout. Guinness has a great malty flavour, which I love to use in bread and I find it works well in a fruit cake too. It lends sweetness and a distinctive taste.

170g raisins
170g sultanas
170g currants
200ml Irish stout, such as Guinness, Beamish or Murphy's
175g unsalted butter
175g dark muscovado sugar
3 large eggs
170g wholemeal self-raising flour
170g self-raising flour
1 tsp ground mixed spice
75g chopped mixed candied peel
Grated zest of 1 lemon
Grated zest of 1 orange

EQUIPMENT
A deep 20cm springform cake tin

STEP PHOTOGRAPHS OVERLEAF

1. Put the dried fruit in a saucepan, pour over the stout and heat gently until it comes to the boil. Remove from the heat, cover and leave to cool completely.

2. Heat the oven to 150°C/Gas 2. Grease a deep 20cm springform cake tin and line the base and sides with baking parchment, extending the parchment high above the rim to protect the cake during cooking.

3. Beat the butter and sugar together until fluffy, then beat in the eggs one at a time, adding a spoonful of the flour with the last egg, if necessary, to prevent curdling. Sift in the remaining flours and the mixed spice and fold them in with a large metal spoon or spatula.

4. Fold in the soaked fruit, including any stout that hasn't been absorbed. Finally mix in the candied peel and lemon and orange zest. If the mixture is very stiff, add a little more stout or a splash of milk.

5. Transfer the mixture to the prepared tin and level the surface. Bake for 2–2¼ hours, until a skewer inserted in the centre comes out clean. If the top gets too dark before the cake is done, cover it with a sheet of foil.

6. Leave to cool in the tin before turning out. This cake should keep for a couple of weeks, wrapped in baking parchment and stored in an airtight tin.

Adding the first egg to the creamed butter and brown sugar mixture.

Grating the lemon zest over the cake mixture, using a fine Microplane grater.

Folding the soaked fruit into the cake mixture, using a spatula.

Spooning the cake mixture into the parchment-lined cake tin.

Incorporating the citrus zest and candied peel.

OAT BISCUITS

MAKES 18–20

These plain, semi-sweet biscuits are similar to digestives in flavour but with a rougher texture. They work equally well with a cup of tea or a piece of cheese.

75g unsalted butter

50g caster sugar

1 medium egg, lightly beaten

150g wholemeal flour

75g rolled oats

½ tsp salt

½ tsp baking powder

EQUIPMENT

A 6cm pastry cutter

1. Heat the oven to 200°C/Gas 6. Line 2 baking trays with baking parchment.

2. Put the butter and sugar in a bowl and beat until pale and fluffy. Beat in the egg, then add the flour, oats, salt and baking powder and mix to form a rough dough.

3. Turn the dough out onto a floured surface and knead briefly until smooth. Roll out to a 5mm thickness and stamp out rounds with a 6cm cutter, gathering together the offcuts and rolling them out again to cut more.

4. Using a palette knife, transfer the dough rounds to the prepared trays and bake for about 10 minutes, until lightly coloured and firm to the touch.

5. Leave on the trays for a few minutes, then transfer to a wire rack to cool. The biscuits will keep well in an airtight tin.

SCOTLAND

ISLE OF LEWIS

SKYE

ISLAY

STRANRAER•

DUMFRIES & GALLOWAY

Ecclefechan •

BORDERS

•Selkirk

•KILMARNOCK

•GLASGOW

EAST LOTHIAN

EDINBURGH•Tantallon Castle

•St Fillans

•OBAN

FORT WILLIAM•

PERTHSHIRE

DUNDEE
•

ANGUS

CAIRNGORMS

•INVERNESS

DINGWALL•

•ULLAPOOL

THURSO
•

Renowned for being talented bakers, the Scots are also famous for their sweet tooth. Perhaps it is the challenging climate that makes them partial to a square of tablet (the Scottish version of fudge), a finger or two of shortbread, a ginger biscuit or a slab of rich fruit cake. Small treats such as these, washed down with a cup of tea, make the cold that little bit more bearable.

Scotland might be generally chillier than the rest of the British Isles but it is also blessed with some of the most staggeringly beautiful countryside, which yields not just top-class game and fish but delicately scented heather honey and juicy, flavoursome raspberries and wild berries. Despite the Scottish love of sweet treats, the traditional diet is frugal and sustaining, based most famously on oats but also on barley and wheat. It has this in common with Ireland, and many of its bakes, such as griddle scones and oat bread, are similar.

There are so many baked goods that seem to exemplify Scotland: shortbread, of course, but also bannocks, scones, oatcakes, Dundee cake, gingerbread… it's no wonder that Scotland was described by Robert Burns as 'the land o' cakes'. Centuries ago, the definition of cake would have included loaves of bread, which were shaped as a shallow round, and also thin griddle cakes such as oatcakes.

Oatcakes date back hundreds of years, yet seem just as relevant to our diet today as they did to the soldiers who used to carry a bag of oatmeal and a metal plate with them, so they could make up a batch with water and cook them over a fire as needed.

Other Scottish cakes, though, are more elaborate, and require rather more skill. The Scottish cookery writer F. Marian McNeill said, 'Every Scotswoman is born with a rolling pin under her arm.' It's not just the pies and pastries that require an experienced hand, but shortbread and scones, which need a light touch and an ability to judge the consistency of the dough.

Anyone who has ever been in Scotland for Hogmanay over the New Year will know how seriously it is taken. Black bun (page 279) – a rich fruit cake wrapped in pastry – is reserved for the occasion. The only way to enjoy it, of course, is with a dram or two of whisky as you toast the year ahead.

500g strong white bread flour

80g unsalted butter, diced

150g Cheddar cheese, grated

1 small red onion, finely
chopped

2 tsp chopped chives

2 medium eggs

1 tsp salt

5 tsp baking powder

250ml milk

TO FINISH

1 egg, lightly beaten, to glaze

25g Parmesan cheese, freshly
grated

EQUIPMENT

A 7cm pastry cutter

**STEP PHOTOGRAPHS
OVERLEAF**

Like other professional bakers, I use strong flour for scones; it gives them greater strength and structure. As long as you handle the dough lightly and don't roll it out too thinly, you'll be rewarded with an excellent rise and light, fluffy scones. Serve these savoury scones with soup for lunch, or at teatime. They are best eaten on the day they're made, or you can freeze them.

1. Heat the oven to 220°C/Gas 7.

2. Put 450g of the flour into a bowl, add the butter and rub it in with your fingertips until the mixture resembles breadcrumbs. Add the cheese, onion, chives, eggs, salt and baking powder and mix gently with a wooden spoon.

3. Add half the milk and turn the mixture gently to combine. Add the remaining milk a little at a time, bringing the mix together with your hand to form a very soft, sticky dough. You may not need all the milk.

4. Dust a work surface with most of the remaining 50g flour. Tip the dough onto it and sprinkle the rest of the flour on top. Fold the dough in half, then turn it 90° and repeat. Do this a few times until all the flour is incorporated and you have a smooth dough. It will also introduce air into the mixture, which will make the scones light. If the mixture is too sticky to handle, dust your hands with flour. Try not to overwork the dough.

5. Dust the work surface and dough lightly with flour, then gently roll the dough out to a 2.5cm thickness. Using a 7cm pastry cutter dipped in flour, stamp out rounds and place them on a baking tray. Don't twist the cutter, just press firmly, then lift up and gently press the dough out. Press together the trimmings and re-roll to make more scones.

6. Brush the tops of the scones with beaten egg and sprinkle with the Parmesan. Bake for 15 minutes, until risen and golden brown. Transfer to a wire rack to cool.

Bringing the scone mixture together with your hand to form a very soft, sticky dough.

Incorporating the remaining 50g flour into the wet, sticky dough on the work surface.

Stamping out rounds from the thickly rolled out dough, by pressing a floured 7cm cutter straight down through the dough (without twisting it).

Gathering together the trimmings, ready to press together and re-roll to make more scones.

SCOTLAND

Brushing the top of the scones with beaten egg before sprinkling with grated Parmesan.

SULTANA SCONE RING

MAKES 8 TRIANGLES

250g strong white bread flour
A pinch of salt
40g unsalted butter, diced
40g caster sugar
60g sultanas
1 medium egg, plus 1 egg,
    lightly beaten, to glaze
2 tsp baking powder
125ml milk

Scone rings are traditional in Scotland and the North. In the past they would have been made from oatmeal or barley, both of which thrive in Scotland. Shaped into a round and marked into triangles for baking, these scones retain moisture well and are particularly soft and fluffy when pulled apart.

1. Heat the oven to 220°C/Gas 7. Line a baking tray with baking parchment.

2. Put 225g of the flour into a bowl with the salt. Add the butter and rub it in with your fingertips until the mixture resembles breadcrumbs. Add the sugar, sultanas, egg and baking powder and mix gently with a wooden spoon.

3. Add half the milk and keep turning the mixture gently to combine. Add the remaining milk a little at a time, bringing everything together to form a very soft dough. You might not need all the milk.

4. Dust a work surface with most of the remaining 25g flour. Tip the dough out onto it and sprinkle the rest of the flour on top. The mixture will be wet and sticky. Fold the dough in half, then turn it 90° and repeat. Do this a few times until the remaining flour is all incorporated and you have a smooth dough. It will also introduce air into the mixture, which will make the scones light. If the mixture is too sticky to handle, dust your hands with flour. Try not to overwork the dough.

5. Form the dough into a rough circle about 2.5cm thick and lift it onto the lined baking tray. Mark it into 8 triangles, cutting deeply through the dough so the knife touches the baking tray.

6. Brush the top of the dough with beaten egg to glaze and bake for 20 minutes, until the scones are risen and golden brown.

A bannock usually refers to a large, flattish round loaf. In the past it would have been a simple unleavened bread baked on a griddle but the Selkirk bannock, from the Borders town of the same name, is a sweet, buttery dough, enriched with sultanas and candied peel and baked in the oven. An egg glaze gives the characteristic glossy, burnished crust. Best served sliced and buttered, for breakfast or tea.

500g strong white bread flour

5g salt

60g caster sugar

7g sachet instant yeast

80g unsalted butter, diced and softened

175ml milk

125ml water

200g sultanas

50g mixed candied peel

1 egg, lightly beaten with 1 tsp milk or water, to glaze

STEP PHOTOGRAPHS
OVERLEAF

1. Put the flour in a large bowl and add the salt and sugar on one side, the yeast on the other. Add the butter to the centre of the bowl and rub it into the flour with your fingertips.

2. Add the milk and half the water, then turn the mixture round with the fingers of one hand. Add the remaining water a little at a time, continuing to mix until you have taken in all the flour from the side of the bowl and the dough is soft and slightly sticky; you might not need all the water.

3. Turn the dough out onto a lightly floured surface. Knead the dough well for at least 5 minutes, working through the initial wet stage until it is smooth and no longer sticky.

4. Lightly oil the bowl, return the dough to it and cover with cling film. Leave to rise for at least an hour, until doubled in size — this will take anything from 1–3 hours.

5. Line a baking tray with baking parchment. Add the sultanas and candied peel to the dough and knead them in. Tip the dough out onto a lightly floured surface and knead briefly.

6. Shape the dough into a bannock — a round dome about 20cm in diameter. Place on the prepared baking tray; put into a plastic bag and leave to prove for about an hour, until doubled in size.

7. Heat the oven to 220°C/Gas 7. Brush the top and sides of the bannock with beaten egg and bake for 10 minutes. Lower the oven setting to 190°C/Gas 5 and bake for a further 25 minutes, until the loaf is a deep brown colour and sounds hollow when tapped underneath. Transfer to a wire rack to cool.

Bringing the soft and slightly sticky dough together with the hand.

Kneading the dough on a lightly floured surface through the initial wet stage.

Continuing to knead the dough by stretching it and tucking the top into the middle, until it is smooth and no longer sticky.

Uncovering the bowl of risen dough, now twice its original volume.

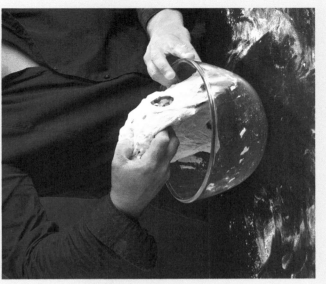

Kneading the sultanas and candied peel into the risen dough.

Lifting the dough out onto a lightly floured surface, ready to knead a little more and shape.

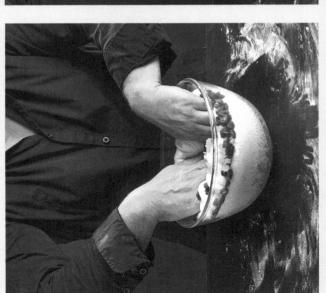

Forming the dough into a dome, about 20cm in diameter, to create the classic bannock shape.

Brushing the top and sides of the proved bannock with beaten egg to glaze, just before baking.

MARMALADE CHEESECAKE WITH WHISKY ORANGES

SERVES 8

Two of Scotland's most celebrated products – marmalade and whisky – come together in this contemporary recipe. Marmalade gives the cheesecake an interesting flavour twist and whisky-macerated oranges are a lovely contrast to the light, creamy texture.

BASE

250g ginger biscuits
120g unsalted butter, melted

FILLING

350g ricotta cheese
350g full-fat cream cheese
2 tbsp cornflour
100g caster sugar
4 medium eggs
4 tbsp thick-cut orange marmalade
Grated zest of 1 orange

WHISKY ORANGES

3 large oranges
100g caster sugar
75ml water
1 tbsp whisky

EQUIPMENT

A 23cm springform cake tin

1. Heat the oven to 170°C/Gas 3. Lightly butter a 23cm springform cake tin.

2. For the base, blitz the ginger biscuits in a food processor until finely ground. Add the melted butter and process again until thoroughly combined. Press this mixture evenly over the base of the tin. Chill to firm up while you make the filling.

3. Put the ricotta, cream cheese, cornflour and sugar in a large bowl and beat with an electric whisk until well combined. Beat in the eggs, then mix in the marmalade and orange zest.

4. Pour the mixture over the biscuit base and bake on a low oven shelf for 35–40 minutes, until the cheesecake is set around the edges but still slightly wobbly in the middle.

5. Turn off the oven and leave the cheesecake inside with the door ajar until it is cool (this helps to ensure the top doesn't split). When the cheesecake is completely cold, place it in the fridge.

6. Meanwhile, to prepare the whisky oranges, cut the peel off the oranges with a sharp knife, removing all the white pith. Now cut out the orange segments from between the membranes; it's best to do this over a bowl to catch the juice.

7. Put the sugar and water in a small pan and bring to the boil, stirring until the sugar dissolves. Simmer for 2–3 minutes, then remove from the heat and add the orange segments, together with any juice. Stir in the whisky and leave to cool.

8. Unmould the cheesecake and serve cut into wedges, with the whisky oranges spooned over.

ST FILLANS' PUDDING

SERVES 6

St Fillans is a tiny village in Perthshire with a population of around 225 people and a colony of fairies. Impossible, you scoff, but in 2005 villagers were scandalised when a housing developer planned to move a rock, because they feared it would kill the fairies living under it. After a tussle with the local community council, the development was redesigned and the fairies were left in peace. This pudding is quite similar to a fruit cobbler. Serve with plenty of thick cream – fairy dust optional.

650g cooking apples, peeled, cored and sliced
30g caster sugar
¼ tsp ground cinnamon
3 tbsp water
A handful of raspberries (optional)

TOPPING
225g plain flour
1 tsp baking powder
1 tsp cream of tartar
110g caster sugar
80g unsalted butter, diced
2 medium eggs
40–60ml milk
1 tbsp demerara sugar

EQUIPMENT
A 900ml baking dish

1. Heat the oven to 180°C/Gas 4. Butter an ovenproof dish, about 900ml in capacity.

2. Peel, core and slice the apples and put them into a saucepan. Add the sugar, cinnamon and water, then cover and cook gently, stirring occasionally, until the apples are just beginning to break down. Stir in the raspberries, if using, and transfer the fruit to the prepared dish.

3. For the topping, put the flour, baking powder and cream of tartar into a bowl and stir in the sugar. Rub in the butter with your fingertips until the mixture resembles fine breadcrumbs. Stir in the eggs and enough milk to make a thick batter.

4. Drop spoonfuls of the batter on top of the fruit and spread it out gently. Sprinkle with the demerara sugar and bake for 25–30 minutes, until the topping is risen and golden brown.

TREACLE SPONGE PUDDING

SERVES 6

Treacle is a little riff running through Scots baking. You'll come across treacle scones, treacle toffee, treacle in gingerbreads and fruit cakes and, best of all, treacle puddings. Unlike in England, where treacle often refers to golden syrup (think treacle tart), it usually means the black stuff in Scotland. This pudding combines the two to give the best of both worlds. It's deliciously rich and not unlike sticky toffee pudding. You've just got to have it with custard.

115g golden syrup
1 tbsp black treacle
100g unsalted butter, well softened
100g caster sugar
3 medium eggs
110g self-raising flour
1 tsp baking powder

EQUIPMENT
A 1 litre pudding basin

1. Butter a 1 litre pudding basin. Spoon 50g of the golden syrup into the bottom of the basin.

2. Put the remaining syrup into a large bowl and add all the other ingredients. Beat together using an electric whisk: start off slowly, then gradually increase the speed and mix for 2 minutes until all the ingredients are well combined. Pour the mixture into the pudding basin, on top of the golden syrup.

3. Place a piece of baking parchment over a sheet of foil and make a large pleat in the middle, folding both sheets together (this allows the pudding to expand as it cooks). Put the parchment and foil on top of the pudding basin, foil-side up, and secure with string, looping the end of the string over the top of the pudding and tying it to form a handle that will enable you to lift the pudding in and out of the saucepan.

4. Put the basin in a large steamer, cover and steam for 1¼ hours, topping up the boiling water if necessary so it doesn't boil dry. (If you don't have a steamer, stand the basin in a large saucepan and pour in enough boiling water to come halfway up the side of the basin, then cover the pan with a lid and simmer for 1¼ hours, topping up the water as necessary.)

5. Remove the pudding basin from the pan, take off the foil and parchment and run the tip of a small, sharp knife around the edge of the pudding to help release it. Invert a large plate over the top of the basin and then turn both over to unmould the pudding. Serve piping hot with custard, or cream.

ECCLEFECHAN BUTTER TARTS

If you've never had these before, you're in for a treat. They are named after the village of Ecclefechan in Dumfries and Galloway. A rich, toffeeish confection of dried fruit, nuts, butter and dark sugar, they include a surprise spoonful of vinegar, which adds a little kick and takes the edge off the sweetness. I consider them a posh version of a Cumberland rum nicky, a northern tart made with ginger, rum, brown sugar and dried fruit.

PASTRY

200g plain flour
2 tbsp icing sugar
100g cold unsalted butter, diced
1 medium egg
1 tsp lemon juice
2–3 tsp ice-cold water

FILLING

150g dark soft brown sugar
2 medium eggs
100g unsalted butter, melted
1 tbsp sherry vinegar
200g mixed dried fruit
25g walnuts, chopped
25g pecan nuts, chopped

EQUIPMENT

A 12-hole muffin tray
A 10cm pastry cutter

STEP PHOTOGRAPHS OVERLEAF

1. To make the pastry, put the flour and icing sugar into a bowl and add the butter. Rub it in lightly with your fingertips until the mixture resembles fine breadcrumbs. Mix the egg with the lemon juice and 2 tsp water. Add to the mixture and stir in with a round-bladed knife, adding another 1 tsp water if necessary. When the dough begins to stick together, gently knead it into a smooth ball. (Alternatively you can make it in a food processor, blitzing the flour, icing sugar and butter together, then adding the liquid.)

2. Wrap the pastry in cling film and chill for at least 30 minutes. Heat the oven to 200°C/Gas 6.

3. Roll out the pastry on a lightly floured surface to a 2–3mm thickness. Using a 10cm cutter, cut out 12 circles and use them to line a muffin tray.

4. For the filling, beat the brown sugar with the eggs, then beat in the melted butter. Add the vinegar and dried fruit and mix well, then divide the mixture between the pastry cases.

5. Mix the walnuts and pecans together and sprinkle them over the tarts. Bake for 15–20 minutes, until the pastry is golden and the filling has only a slight wobble.

6. Place the muffin tray on a wire rack to cool slightly. It is easiest to remove the tarts when they are still slightly warm.

Rolling out the rested pastry on a lightly floured surface to a 2–3mm thickness.

Pressing the pastry rounds into the muffin tray moulds to shape the cases.

Sprinkling the chopped walnuts and pecans over the filling before baking.

Cutting out rounds for the pastry cases, using a 10cm cutter.

Spooning the toffeeish dried fruit filling into the pastry cases.

RASPBERRY CRUMBLE CAKE

MAKES A LARGE SLAB CAKE

The Scottish climate is ideal for growing raspberries: a fair amount of rain and gentle sun allow the berries to ripen slowly, giving the flavour plenty of time to develop. They feature in cranachan, the famous Scottish dessert of whipped cream, honey, whisky, toasted oatmeal and raspberries, all layered in a glass.

This gorgeous crumble cake is an excellent way of using up a small quantity of fruit and it's very quick to make. You could add 1 tsp ground cinnamon to the crumble, if you like — it has a real affinity with raspberries.

225g plain flour
A pinch of salt
2 tsp baking powder
110g caster sugar
30ml sunflower oil
1 large egg
1 tsp vanilla extract
120ml milk
170g raspberries

CRUMBLE
375g plain flour
175g light soft brown sugar
225g unsalted butter, melted

TO FINISH
Icing sugar, for dusting

EQUIPMENT
A 26 x 20cm baking tin

1. Heat the oven to 170°C/Gas 3. Grease a 26 x 20cm baking tin and line the base and sides with baking parchment.

2. Put the flour, salt and baking powder into a large bowl and stir in the sugar. In a separate bowl or a jug, whisk together the oil, egg, vanilla and milk.

3. Pour the liquid onto the dry ingredients and stir until well combined. Gently fold in the raspberries, then spoon the mixture into the prepared tin and spread evenly.

4. To make the crumble, mix the flour and brown sugar together in a large bowl, then stir in the melted butter until the mixture forms large crumbs.

5. Sprinkle the crumble topping evenly over the cake mixture in the tin. Bake for 25–30 minutes, until a skewer inserted in the centre comes out clean.

6. Leave the cake to cool in the tin, then dust with icing sugar and cut into squares to serve.

BLACK BUN

MAKES 1

Originally developed for Christmas, this rich, moist fruity treat is especially popular at the New Year Hogmanay celebrations. Make it a few weeks in advance if possible and store it in an airtight tin so it has time to mature. Serve with a glass of whisky.

1. Heat the oven to 180°C/Gas 4. Grease a 900g loaf tin (about 10 x 20cm base measurement) with lard and line the base and ends with a long strip of baking parchment that overhangs the short ends. This makes it easier to remove the loaf after baking.

2. For the filling, mix all the ingredients together in a large bowl and set aside.

3. To make the pastry, mix the flours together in a bowl and rub in the butter with your fingertips until the mix resembles fine breadcrumbs. Put the water, salt and lard in a saucepan and heat until the lard has melted and the water just comes to the boil. Pour it into the flour mixture and mix with a wooden spoon. Tip out onto a floured surface and knead briefly until smooth.

4. Cut off about a quarter of the pastry and set aside, keeping it covered with cling film. Roll out the remaining pastry to a 6–7mm thickness – work as quickly as you can, as the pastry will become crumbly as it cools.

5. Line the prepared tin with the rolled-out pastry, pressing it gently into the corners and smoothing it out as necessary. Leave the excess pastry hanging over the edges of the tin. Spoon the filling inside and press down lightly.

6. Roll out the remaining pastry to fit the top of the tin. Dampen the edges with water, place it on top of the filling and press the edges together to seal. Trim away the excess pastry and crimp the edges. Make 3 slits in the top to allow steam to escape.

7. Brush the top with beaten egg and bake for 2 hours, covering the top loosely with foil after an hour or so if it becomes too dark. Leave to cool in the tin before turning out.

HOT-WATER PASTRY

450g plain flour
100g strong white bread flour
75g unsalted butter, diced
200ml water
½ tsp salt
100g lard, diced
1 egg, lightly beaten, to glaze

FILLING

200g plain flour
400g raisins
200g sultanas
½ tsp ground cinnamon
½ tsp ground allspice
½ tsp ground mixed spice
100g dark muscovado sugar
80g almonds, chopped
50g walnuts, chopped
½ tsp bicarbonate of soda
1 egg
2 tbsp whisky
3 tbsp milk
Grated zest of 1 orange and juice of ½ orange

EQUIPMENT

A 900g loaf tin

STEP PHOTOGRAPHS
OVERLEAF

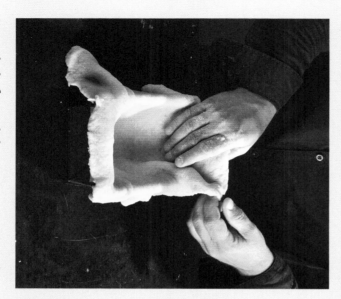

Rolling out the pastry to a large sheet, 6–7cm thick, working quickly as the pastry will become crumbly and difficult to handle as it cools.

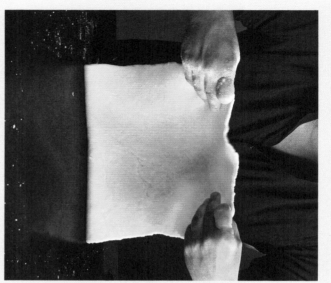

Checking that the pastry sheet is large enough to line the base and sides of the tin.

Lining the loaf tin with the pastry, pressing it gently into the corners and against the sides.

Spooning the spiced fruit and nut filling into the hot-water pastry case.

Trimming the pastry away from the edge of the loaf tin, using a small, sharp knife.

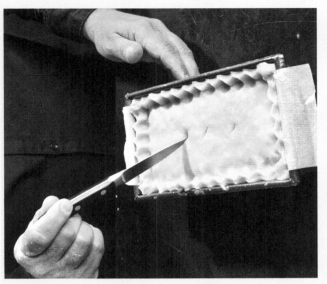

Making 3 slits in the top of the pastry to allow steam to escape during baking.

Lifting the pastry lid over the top of the filling.

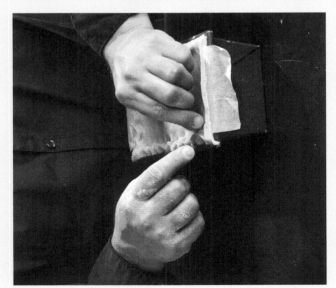

Crimping the pastry edges together between the forefinger and thumb, to seal and create a decorative edge.

MARMALADE CAKE

MAKES A 20CM CAKE

The best-known story about marmalade is that James Keiller, a Dundee shopkeeper, bought some oranges from a Spanish ship docked in the port in the 1700s and ended up with the bitter Seville variety by mistake. His mother, Janet, seized the opportunity to invent marmalade – a happy variation on the 'if life gives you lemons, make lemonade' principle.

Not only is marmalade great on toast, it's also an easy way to make a flavoursome cake. This is also very good made with lime marmalade and a lime icing.

175g unsalted butter, softened
175g caster sugar
3 large eggs
175g self-raising flour
110g Seville orange marmalade

TO FINISH (OPTIONAL)
Caster sugar, for sprinkling
Grated zest of 1 small orange

ICING (OPTIONAL)
200g icing sugar
Finely grated zest of 1 small orange, plus about 25ml juice

EQUIPMENT
A 20cm springform cake tin

1. Heat the oven to 180°C/Gas 4. Grease a 20cm springform cake tin and line the base with baking parchment.

2. Put the butter and sugar in a bowl and beat together until light and fluffy. Beat in the eggs one at a time, adding a spoonful of the flour with the last egg if necessary, to prevent curdling. Sift in the remaining flour and fold it in, using a large metal spoon or spatula. Finally fold in the marmalade.

3. Transfer the mixture to the prepared tin and level the surface. Bake for about 40 minutes, until the cake is well risen and a skewer inserted in the centre comes out clean. Leave in the tin for 10 minutes, then turn out onto a wire rack to cool.

4. For a simple finish, sprinkle caster sugar over the top of the cake and scatter over some orange zest.

5. Or, to make the icing instead, mix the icing sugar with the orange zest and enough orange juice to make a fairly thick icing. Spread it over the top of the cooled cake and leave to set.

CHOCOLATE CHIP PETTICOAT TAILS

MAKES 8 LARGE TRIANGLES

Petticoat tails supposedly resemble the shape of a bell-hoop crinoline petticoat — though there is also a theory that the name is a corruption of *petites gatelles*, little cakes brought from France to Scotland by Mary, Queen of Scots. I favour the petticoat theory over the idea of a French import.

I've cheated slightly here by pressing the mixture into a fluted tart tin to give it an attractively shaped edge, but you could put it in a plain round tin and flute the edge by hand. Traditionally a small circle is cut out of the centre of the shortbread round before baking, to avoid messy breakages from the pointed edges.

1. Heat the oven to 150°C/Gas 2. Lightly grease a 20cm fluted tart tin with butter.

2. Put the butter and sugar in a large bowl and cream together until light and fluffy. Add the flour, semolina, salt and chocolate chips and bring everything together to form a dough. Take care not to overwork the mixture.

3. Press the mixture into the prepared tart tin and prick it all over with a fork. Place on a low shelf in the oven and bake for 30–40 minutes. The shortbread should be very pale.

4. As you take the shortbread from the oven, sprinkle the surface with caster sugar. Cut into 8 triangles while still warm. Leave to cool in the tin completely before removing.

100g unsalted butter
55g caster sugar, plus extra
   for sprinkling
125g plain flour
20g semolina (or ground rice)
A pinch of salt
55g chocolate chips

EQUIPMENT
A 20cm fluted tart tin

COCONUT FLAPJACKS

MAKES 12–16

These flapjacks use coconut and two types of oats to give a soft, chewy texture. Ground almonds help keep them moist. The recipe makes a good base for all sorts of additions — dried fruit, chocolate chips or crystallised ginger would all work well.

200g unsalted butter
75g caster sugar
200g golden syrup
150g jumbo oats
150g quick-cook oats
50g desiccated coconut
50g ground almonds

EQUIPMENT
A 25 x 20cm baking tin

1. Heat the oven to 170°C/Gas 3. Line the base and sides of a 25 x 20cm baking tin with baking parchment.

2. Put the butter, sugar and golden syrup in a saucepan and heat gently until melted.

3. In a large bowl, mix the oats, coconut and ground almonds together. Make a well in the centre and pour in the melted ingredients. Stir until thoroughly combined.

4. Tip the mixture into the prepared tin and level the surface. Bake for 25–30 minutes, until bubbling round the edges but still slightly soft in the centre.

5. Cut the flapjack into bars in the tin while still warm, then leave until cold before removing.

TANTALLON CAKES

MAKES 18–20

Tantallon Castle in East Lothian gives its name to these delicious shortbread biscuits (not cakes after all). Good though they are, they make a surprisingly low-key tribute to one of Scotland's most formidable fortifications, built in the 14th century and home to the powerful and ruthless 'Red Douglases', the Earls of Angus. Cromwell laid waste to the castle in 1651 and it now stands in ruins. If you visit, be sure to take a camera. There are at least two instances of ghostly figures in Tudor dress showing up in pictures.

1. Beat the butter and icing sugar together until light and fluffy in a bowl, then beat in the egg yolk, followed by the lemon zest.

2. Sift the flour, cornflour and bicarbonate of soda together. Stir them into the butter and sugar mixture a spoonful at a time, then bring the mixture together into a dough and knead briefly until smooth.

3. Line 2 baking trays with baking parchment. Roll out the dough on a lightly floured surface to a 5mm thickness. Using a 6.5cm fluted cutter, stamp out rounds and place them on the lined baking trays, pressing the trimmings together and re-rolling them to make more biscuits as necessary.

4. Prick the biscuits all over with a fork and chill for 30 minutes; this helps prevent them spreading in the oven. Heat the oven to 180°C/Gas 4.

5. Bake the biscuits for 10–12 minutes, until they are just starting to colour. Leave them on the baking trays for 5 minutes, then transfer to a wire rack to cool. Dust with icing sugar before serving, if you like.

100g unsalted butter, softened
100g icing sugar, plus extra for dusting (optional)
1 large egg yolk
Grated zest of ½ lemon
100g plain flour
100g cornflour
¼ tsp bicarbonate soda

EQUIPMENT
A 6.5cm pastry cutter

OATCAKES

15g butter

15g lard

60ml water

60g fine oatmeal, plus extra for dusting

170g medium oatmeal

½ tsp salt

A pinch of baking powder

EQUIPMENT

A flat griddle (or large heavy-based frying pan)

A 7.5cm pastry cutter

STEP PHOTOGRAPHS OVERLEAF

Oatcakes are one of the most ancient cooked foods. They've been enjoyed in Scotland for centuries, at breakfast, dinner and tea. Dr Johnson was famously unimpressed by the Scots diet, defining oats in his dictionary as 'a grain, which in England is generally given to horses, but in Scotland supports the people'. I'm not sure he could afford to be so dismissive now that oats are recognised as one of the healthiest foods around.

These oatcakes are cooked twice – first on a griddle, then in a low oven – to make sure they are really dry and crisp. A lovely addition to your cheeseboard.

1. Put the butter, lard and water in a small saucepan and melt over a gentle heat.

2. Put the fine and medium oatmeal, salt and baking powder in a bowl and stir together. Add the melted butter mixture and mix to form a paste.

3. Dust a work surface with oatmeal and roll out the mixture to a 3mm thickness. Stamp out rounds with a 7.5cm pastry cutter, then re-roll the trimmings and cut out more oatcakes. If the trimmings are too dry, add a little more melted butter to bind.

4. Heat the oven to 140°C/Gas 1. Place a flat griddle or a large, heavy-based frying pan over a medium heat.

5. When the griddle is hot, grease it lightly with buttered paper. Cook the oatcakes, in batches if necessary, for 4–5 minutes on one side only. When they are golden brown underneath, transfer them to a wire rack.

6. Once all the oatcakes are cooked, stand the wire rack on a baking tray and place in the oven for 30 minutes to dry out the oatcakes completely. Store in an airtight tin.

Stirring the warm melted mixture into the oatmeal mixture.

Flattening the mixture on the work surface, to make it easier to roll.

Gathering the trimmings from between the stamped-out 7.5cm rounds, to re-roll and cut more oatcakes.

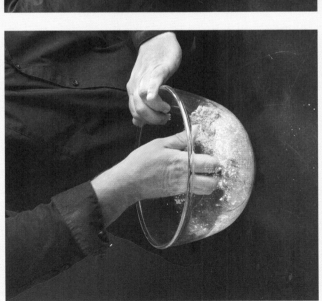

Gathering the mixture with one hand to form a paste.

Rolling out the dough evenly, to a 3mm thickness.

PARLIES

MAKES 20

65g unsalted butter
40g black treacle
25g golden syrup
65g dark soft brown sugar
250g plain flour
1 tsp ground ginger
1 tsp grated nutmeg

Biscuits have a strong heritage in Scotland. Parlies is short for parliament cakes, a type of hard gingerbread that used to be eaten by the lawyers of Parliament Square in Edinburgh during their midday break. Traditionally these thin, crisp, ginger biscuits are square, but you could, of course, cut other shapes if you prefer.

1. Heat the oven to 170°C/Gas 3. Line 2 baking trays with baking parchment.

2. Put the butter, treacle, golden syrup and sugar in a pan and heat gently until melted.

3. Mix the flour, ginger and nutmeg together in a bowl. Stir in the melted ingredients to make a dough, then leave to cool.

4. Roll out the dough on a lightly floured surface to about a 5mm thickness. Cut into 6cm squares and place on the lined trays. Bake for 15–20 minutes, until firm to the touch.

5. Leave the biscuits on the baking trays for a few minutes to allow them to cool slightly and firm up, then transfer to a wire rack to cool completely.

ACKNOWLEDGEMENTS

This book could not have been written without a very special team.

Firstly a huge thanks to Claire Bassano, whose creative input and dedication to the recipes has been fantastic. Also to Jane Middleton for her patience with me during the writing of the book. Sarah Gardiner and Yasmin Othman, thank you for your hours of weighing up ingredients and baking. To Janet Illsley on the editorial side, thank you.

In the Bloomsbury editorial team, who are so supportive and are the best (this is my fourth book with them), a special thank you to Natalie Bellos, Xa Shaw Stewart and Alison Glossop, and also to Marina Asenjo.

To Peter Dawson and Namkwan Cho for the design of this beautiful book, thank you.

A special thanks goes to the best photographer I've worked with, Peter Cassidy, and to Róisín Nield for the perfect prop styling.

To my agents Geraldine Woods, Anna Bruce and Kate Cooper, thank you. Guys, what a team!

Huge thanks and love to my wife Alexandra for her support, and to my grown-up boy Joshua.

INDEX

First published in Great Britain 2014

Text © Paul Hollywood
Photography © Peter Cassidy
Illustration © Jeremy Sancha/CIA

The moral right of the author has been asserted

Bloomsbury Publishing Plc
50 Bedford Square
London WC1B 3DP

bloomsbury.com

Bloomsbury is a trademark of Bloomsbury Publishing Plc

Bloomsbury Publishing, London, New Delhi, New York and Sydney

A CIP catalogue record for this book is available from the British Library

ISBN 978 1 4088 4648 3

10 9 8 7 6 5 4 3 2 1

Project editor: Janet Illsley
Design: Peter Dawson, Namkwan Cho gradedesign.com
Photography: Peter Cassidy
Food editor: Jane Middleton
Recipe development consultant and food stylist: Claire Bassano
Food stylists: Sarah Gardiner and Yasmin Othman
Props stylist: Róisín Nield
Index: Hilary Bird

Printed and bound in Germany by Mohn Media

MIX
Paper from
responsible sources
FSC
www.fsc.org
FSC® C011124